Praise for *The Romance of Religion*

"This book is witty, whimsical, and deadly serious. With panache and aplomb, Dwight Longenecker sets out to prove that Christianity is, in every sense of the word, fabulous. And does he succeed in his quest? I encourage you to read it to find out."

—MICHAEL WARD, SENIOR RESEARCH FELLOW, BLACKFRIARS HALL, UNIVERSITY OF OXFORD; PROFESSOR OF APOLOGETICS, HOUSTON BAPTIST UNIVERSITY

"If you've never thought about the Christian faith as romance and story, then this book will introduce you to a whole new way of thinking."

—FRANK VIOLA, AUTHOR OF *GOD'S FAVORITE PLACE ON EARTH*

"Dwight Longenecker has invented a new branch of thought: rollicking theology! Out of the legacy of Chesterton, Lewis, and Tolkien, he gives us images to play with that also pierce like a two-edged sword. . . . A great book to give to skeptics, friends, and exhausted Christians."

—RONDA CHERVIN, PhD, PROFESSOR OF PHILOSOPHY, HOLY APOSTLES COLLEGE AND SEMINARY; CATHOLIC WRITER; EWTN PRESENTER

"We have been living through etics fed by powerful writers, and D   1. As a Christian Romantic inspired   ows that Imagination can be our pat   *gion*, he uses it to bring the Christian faith to life, revealing Christianity to be the adventure, the quest, we have all been looking for."

—STRATFORD CALDECOTT, G. K. CHESTERTON RESEARCH FELLOW AT ST BENET'S HALL, OXFORD; AUTHOR OF *BEAUTY FOR TRUTH'S SAKE* AND *THE POWER OF THE RING*

"I always knew I was a religious romantic; in this book, Dwight Longenecker shows me why, while writing with the paradoxical wit and wisdom of a twenty-first-century G. K. Chesterton. Even if you don't consider yourself a romantic, or a religious person, this book may just make you long to join in what C. S. Lewis called 'the Great Dance.'"

—WILL VAUS, AUTHOR OF *MERE THEOLOGY:*
A GUIDE TO THE THOUGHT OF C. S. LEWIS

"If you've ever thought religion was dull, boring, or irrelevant, think again. *The Romance of Religion* attunes your senses to the wonder and whim lurking behind every Christian doctrine. Here Dwight Longenecker offers theology that sings. His tune captures our longings for heroism and purpose, epic quests and great battles, and reveals how they all point to a fairy tale—one that is true and divine. Read this book, hear this song, and let it sweep you into the Great Adventure. Chesterton would be proud."

—BRANDON VOGT, BLOGGER AND AUTHOR
OF *THE CHURCH AND NEW MEDIA*

"Longenecker is a master storyteller with a penchant for alliteration. A lesser writer might be held captive by the rhythm and rhyme in *The Romance of Religion* and lose sight of the reality. Not so, Dwight Longenecker: his subtitles are catchy, yet imbued with logic—and they drive the reader down the trail of self-realization and off into the sunset, into Love and Light, to become extraordinary by becoming what they were meant to be. I couldn't stop reading."

—KATHY SCHIFFER, SEASONS OF GRACE BLOGGER

"Combining a pastor's knowledge of where people are, and a writer's desire to help them see what they haven't yet seen, and adding a good bit of wit, Dwight Longenecker presents the Christian adventure in a way that can win a hearing among those who don't believe it and help those who do see truths they hadn't seen or seen so clearly."

—DAVID MILLS, EXECUTIVE EDITOR,
FIRST THINGS JOURNAL AND WEBSITE

"Like a crusading preacher of the Middle Ages, Dwight Longenecker stands at the gates of our city, begging us to join him in battle. *The Romance of Religion* trumpets the notes of love, sacrifice, and mystery. In an age where everyone wants to be 'spiritual but not religious,' Longenecker challenges us to take up the cross of the only religion with romance: Christianity."

—TAYLOR MARSHALL, PhD, AUTHOR OF
THE CRUCIFIED RABBI AND PRESIDENT OF
THE NEW SAINT THOMAS INSTITUTE

"In *The Romance of Religion*, Dwight Longenecker invites the reader to gather shield and buckler and ride off with him to discover the romance within the great countercultural quest that is Christianity— a continual fight for life, love, and truth set amid the tilted windmills of modern ideologies, trends, and entertainments. In an era of dark antiheroes like Dexter Morgan and Walter White, Longenecker—with wit, keen literary insight, and a deceptively deft hand—makes the case for old-school, faith-informed heroism, where the way to victory runs counter to the world's understanding, and the depths of our wounds are remarkable not for their power to deter, but for guiding light they emit as we move forward. *The Romance of Religion* brings together magic and superheroes and idols and villains and even the strong, remarkable women without which no great adventure is complete. It makes time spent with any other romance seem less than satisfying, indeed!"

—ELIZABETH SCALIA, AUTHOR OF *STRANGE
GODS: UNMASKING THE IDOLS IN EVERYDAY LIFE*

"Dwight Longenecker's newest book is the perfect antidote to the theologically fuzzy, feel-good rock concert that passes for 'worship' in so many current Christian circles. By reminding the reader that discipleship is meant to be so much wilder, more dangerous, and more unruly than a sermon series or community project, he gets us back to an understanding of Christianity that is beautiful, profound, and fulfilling to the deepest parts of our souls."

—CARI DONALDSON, AUTHOR OF *POPE AWESOME AND
OTHER STORIES* AND BLOGGER AT CLAN-DONALDSON.COM

"From evangelical student to Anglican and Catholic, Dwight Longenecker has lived the spiritual quest for truth, beauty, and goodness, and in *The Romance of Religion* he encourages us to step out of our comfort zones and engage in the great battle. He does so with zest, panache, and wielding the ready sword of wit and wisdom. This is a rumbustious read and a true inspiration."

—Marcus Grodi, founder of the Coming Home Network; author; host of EWTN's *Journeys Home*

"With his customary candor, and in the lively, well-turned phrases for which he is famous, Dwight Longenecker wipes away the cobwebs from the bold claims of orthodox Christianity. He shows the reader how the religious impulse, honestly followed, is not a means of living a dull, respectable life. Instead it is a daunting, life-changing challenge, which we do our best to evade or wish away through a thousand little subterfuges. But he won't let us get away with that. He's in love with the risk required in facing up to Reality—which always exceeds and explodes our man-made categories. This book is a roadmap for a journey into the unknown and the eternal."

—John Zmirak, author of *The Bad Catholic's Guide to the Catechism*

"Many people think of religion as a subject that is either dull or divisive, but in *The Romance of Religion*, Longenecker reveals that it can be exhilarating and romantic. Religion deals with the deepest question in life, the ones that most touch our hearts, and his new book makes a passionate case for why we must fight for goodness, truth, and beauty in religion and in all of life."

—Jimmy Akin, senior apologist, Catholic Answers

THE
ROMANCE
of RELIGION

FIGHTING FOR GOODNESS,
TRUTH, AND BEAUTY

DWIGHT
LONGENECKER

W PUBLISHING GROUP

AN IMPRINT OF THOMAS NELSON

© 2014 Dwight Longenecker

All rights reserved. No portion of this book may be reproduced, stored in a retrieval system, or transmitted in any form or by any means—electronic, mechanical, photocopy, recording, scanning, or other—except for brief quotations in critical reviews or articles, without the prior written permission of the publisher.

Published in Nashville, Tennessee, by W Publishing, an imprint of Thomas Nelson.

Thomas Nelson titles may be purchased in bulk for educational, business, fund-raising, or sales promotional use. For information, please e-mail SpecialMarkets@ ThomasNelson.com.

Excerpts from "East Coker" and "Little Gidding" from *Four Quartets* by T. S. Eliot. Copyright 1940, 1942 by T. S. Eliot; Copyright renewed 1968, 1970 by Esme Valerie Eliot. Reprinted by permission of Houghton Mifflin Harcourt Publishing Company. All rights reserved.

Scripture quotations marked ESV are from The Holy Bible, English Standard Version® (ESV®), copyright © 2001 by Crossway, a publishing ministry of Good News Publishers. Used by permission. All rights reserved.

Scripture quotations marked KJV are from the King James Version. Public domain.

Scripture quotations marked NCV are from The New Century Version®. © 2005 by Thomas Nelson, Inc. Used by permission. All rights reserved.

Scripture quotations marked NIV are from the Holy Bible, New International Version®, NIV®. Copyright © 1973, 1978, 1984, 2011 by Biblica, Inc.™ Used by permission of Zondervan. All rights reserved worldwide. www.zondervan.com

Scripture quotations marked NKJV are from the New King James Version®. © 1982 by Thomas Nelson, Inc. Used by permission. All rights reserved.

Scripture quotations marked NLT are from the Holy Bible, New Living Translation. © 1996, 2004, 2007. Used by permission of Tyndale House Publishers, Inc., Carol Stream, Illinois 60188. All rights reserved.

Scripture quotations marked RSV are from Revised Standard Version of the Bible, copyright 1952 [2nd edition, 1971] by the Division of Christian Education of the National Council of the Churches of Christ in the United States of America. Used by permission. All rights reserved.

Library of Congress Control Number: 2013920597

Printed in the United States of America

14 15 16 17 18 RRD 5 4 3 2 1

To Alison
with love at last

CONTENTS

INTRODUCTION

RESPECTABILITY AND THE HOUSE OF HORRORS

The Need for Table Turning

In one of his stories, Graham Greene said that for every individual there is a moment in childhood when the future opens up and he has an insight that reveals his destiny.

I had just such an experience when I was in the fifth grade. I was riding home from school in a big yellow bus on a fine autumn day; as we lived in the country on the edge of the school district, I rode alone at the back of the bus for nearly thirty minutes every afternoon. I remember sitting and looking out the window at the fall colors in the sort of contemplative mood that comes naturally to children. I was thinking what I would do with my life, and it occurred to me in a flash of quiet inspiration that, while I did not have any idea what I would do with my life, I had a very clear idea what I would not do.

I would not work in an office. I would not be an employee. I would not be a drudge. I would not be a drone or a dromedary. I would not be a mindless worker or a beast of burden. I did not have the faintest idea what I would do, but I knew I would not punch a time clock. I would not sit at a desk, loathing Monday and longing for Friday. I did not mind the thought of making some great and heroic sacrifice, but I would not keep my nose to a grindstone. I would not capitulate. I would not sit timidly at my desk year after year, accumulating money, submitting to a system, and counting the days until I might receive a watch, a handshake, and a retirement check.

With some luck, hard work, and a bit of ingenuity, my dream became my destiny, and I have never been a drudge, a drone, or a dromedary. I've been poor and uncertain of my future. I have turned my back on quislings, rejected promotions, and quit jobs that did not suit me even though they were secure. I've walked out on compromisers and cowards, given a jaunty salute of farewell, and taken the road less traveled. Alas, my insouciance and independence have gotten me into trouble. I am perceived as aloof and arrogant—an unstable upstart, an unpredictable problem, a loose cannon, a piece of the puzzle that does not fit.

All we can do is be true to ourselves, hope for the best, and apologize for our failures.

I can honestly say that I have walked this strange and disturbing pathway through life because of my Sunday school teacher—a demure lady named Betty, who taught me the stories of Jesus using a delightful visual aid called a flannelgraph.

Betty would place cut-out figures of Jesus and the disciples on a flannel-covered board and move them about to illustrate the story. So I learned about Zaccheus, who climbed the sycamore tree, and the boy who gave his lunch to feed five thousand, and Lazarus, who rose like a fearsome mummy from the dead.

It is Betty's fault that I have offended everyone by being arrogant because she also told me the story of Jesus Christ turning over the tables in the temple of Jerusalem. To me this was the most exciting and remarkable story of all. The righteous religious people told me that Jesus turned over the tables because he disapproved of the merchants selling things in church. I think Betty followed their line, because she used notes from a little paperback book.

This, however, never convinced me. I knew the truth. Jesus turned over the tables in the temple because he enjoyed it. He trashed the place. He was angry. He sent the pigeons flying. The sheep and goats went bleating as he gave the thieves a beating. He scattered the proud in their conceit and dashed their little heads against the pavement. The story thrilled me. No longer would I believe only in the gentle Jesus who took little kiddies on his lap and blessed them. No longer would I believe only in the Good Shepherd with yellow hair and clean robes who carried a little lambkin on his shoulders and "home, rejoicing, brought" him.[1] No longer would I believe only in the smiling, suffering, milquetoast, doormat Jesus.

No longer would I believe
only in the smiling, suffering,
milquetoast, doormat Jesus.

I listened more closely to the stories and tried to find traces of my table-turning Jesus elsewhere, and I found him! He saw Peter, Andrew, James, and John being drones and dromedaries and told them to walk away from it all, to leave their nets and follow him. He came walking on the waves one night and dared Peter to do the same. Did he condemn people and tell them to go to hell? Not the poor sinners who were ashamed of themselves anyway, but I was delighted to find that he did thunder and threaten hell. And I was even more delighted to find that it was the religious people he had in his sights. They were a "brood of vipers" and their "father" was "the devil." There was a place reserved for them, he cried, "where the fire is not quenched and the worm dieth not."[2]

"Where the worm dieth not! Where the worm dieth not!" It was horribly real and wonderfully macabre. The tapeworm that gnaws on your insides while you are still alive dieth not. The maggot that consumes your dead flesh dieth not. A vile beast like a moray eel squirms within your empty skull and dieth not. The worm—Smaug—that great dragon of Middle-earth—lurks within your bowels and dieth not. This was the Jesus I could follow: the Jesus who called a boy on a great adventure—the Jesus who expected you to never be a drone or a dromedary—the Jesus who turned over the tables and called people to walk on water and told insufferable religious people they were going where "the fire is not quenched and the worm dieth not."

Then I looked further into the New Testament to see if I could discover other writings that were similarly outrageous and adventuresome. Imagine my delight when I discovered that Saint Paul, whom the preachers presented as a sort of seriously puritanical protestant, turned out to be a man of passion and wild abandon. He was not the dour Sunday school teacher I had been led to expect, but someone who cried in grief that he was a sinful man, who did what he did not want to do and did not do what he wanted to do! That was me too.

He declared that he was throwing off every constraint to run a marathon that he was determined to complete. Like a Shakespearean jester, he spoke in paradox and riddles: "It is when I am most weak that I am most strong!" With a kind of daring insouciance, he defied the worldly drones and drudges by saying that the "foolishness of God is wiser than the wisdom of men!" He shook his fist in the face of Mr. Death and cried, "O death, where is your victory? O death, where is your sting?"[3] In my childhood home the Jacobean cadences of the King James Version struck into my heart the poetry, the passion, and the panache of following the great hero Christ the Lord.

So I determined to follow the Master on this sort of mad, wave-walking adventure. The heroes in our Bible church were the missionaries: men and women who went out to the darkest and most horrible places on earth. They went to the places where the natives' hearts were hardest, their sin saddest, and their darkness deepest. I prayed that I might be sent to a place like that. "Oh, Lord!" I cried, "Send me to a people who shake their fists in your face! Send me to those who are lost in ignorance and pride and swallowed up in the great and miserable swamp called sin! Send me to the vilest and most violent sinners of all." So he sent me to England.

You will imagine my dismay when I went on the adventure and became an Anglican priest, only to find that the tables had been set up again and business in the temple was booming, and that, furthermore, I had committed myself to be one of the very ones he mocked for wearing long robes and being greeted with respect and loving to sit in the best seats in the temple. In addition, they had taken the table turner and turned him into someone else. They had tamed him.

They took the yokel carpenter and country preacher and put him in stained-glass windows and gave him neatly waved hair and splendid robes, which they had bought from the finest ecclesiastical haberdashery. There he was again in the stained-glass windows, sweetly smiling and blessing little children and carrying little lambkins on his shoulder and knocking on doors to come in. In other words, they had remade Jesus in their own image, and even worse, I had become one of them.

They had captured the ragtag revolutionary rabbi and made him respectable. The whole wildfire religion that had captured my imagination as a child had been turned into a kind of wax museum house of horrors. Fake wax dummies—the authority figures of artificial religion—moved robotically as if on some kind of a mechanical merry-go-round. Their smiles were bizarrely permanent, their hair neatly coiffed, their costumes pressed and perfect. They were going through the motions of religion in a gruesome charade like the little dolls who sing "It's a Small World." Wherever I turned, religion had become not real but respectable. It was impossible to escape the horror. I wanted to run screaming from this nightmare world, but wherever I turned I met only more ornate wax figures reaching out to grab me and pull me in and turn me into not just a drone and a dromedary but something far worse: a religiously respectable waxwork Christian—a figure from the house of horrors who might melt in the heat.

Wherever I turned, religion had become not real but respectable.

So I determined to never forsake the boyhood dream. I would not submit. I would continue the wild and foolish adventure. I would play the prophet and continue to follow the Master and turn over the tables. That's what this book is about. It is a call to adventure for those who will hear. It is an attempt to escape the house of horrors that is respectable religion and turn over the tables in the temple once more. It is a call for others to entertain the foolishness of God that is wiser than the wisdom of men; to reject the respectability of religion and embrace the romance of religion.

Some readers may be surprised to learn that I am a Catholic priest and wonder that I have not sought to turn over the tables in that most magnificent and terrible temple of all: the Catholic Church. This is where I must turn the tables on you again, for I have discovered that, indeed, the least respectable church of them all is the Catholic Church. Oh yes, from time to time she has appeared to be respectable. She has sat at the high table and dined with princes and potentates, but history has shown that the alliance never lasts, and she is soon thrown down again among the poor and the lowly. When you study her history closely, you discover that in every age and in nearly every place she has been persecuted by worldlings without and worm eaten by corruption within.

The Catholic Church may appear to be respectable, but

do not be deceived. It is a ruse. It is a clever disguise. Even the most respectable-looking cardinal in his crimson robes is a secret table turner. The mildest-mannered nun is a sly subversive, and the meekest faithful priest in his black robes is an agent provocateur. To be sure, we are not pure. In our army, like every army, there are deserters and traitors and cowards. We are a church of sinners and saints—which is the strange mark of our authenticity. Yes, we have some colossal failures, but think about it: Wouldn't you be even more suspicious of a church where everyone was perfect? Believe me: the Catholic Church has many problems, but being respectable is not one of them.

Although I am a Catholic priest, this book is not an attempt to convert my readers to Catholicism. Instead, it is a call for ordinary people to examine the radical claims of the table-turning teacher from Galilee. It is a call for others to get up out of their fishing boats and to follow the Master. It is an argument for a life that has meaning and purpose—a life of faith that is a glorious adventure or it is nothing at all.

Dwight Longenecker
Greenville, South Carolina
April 2013

The
Foundations
for Fighting

CYRANO OR CYNICISM?

Why Rollicking Romanticism Is Good for You

In a world of useful things, it might seem absurd to write a book in praise of romance. Who needs romance in a world that has been rationalized, economized, mechanized, and computerized? Can romance survive in a world of profit margins and the bottom line? Isn't romance (with its unfulfilled longing) a waste of time in a world where every desire can be gratified cheerfully and cheaply? Can the frail flower of romance live in the winter of a cold and cynical age? Can romance thrive where angels in full flight are shot down with facts and fragile ideals are shattered by the hard stones of reality?

Let's be optimistic. We should never be too convinced by the attitudes and emotions of the age in which we live. When poisonous ideas are universal, the desire for an antidote becomes all the more urgent. Like Achilles, the hero who forgot his heel, or like Icarus who, flying close to the sun, forgot that his wings were made of wax, we should be wary when triumphant ideas seem unassailable, for then there is all the more reason to predict their downfall. Anything that has reached its peak must be on the brink of decline. The bigger a bubble, the more likely it is to burst. Likewise, any process of thought that seems down-and-out is probably about to come up and in. That which has reached its nadir can only go up.

History shows that the pendulum swings back. Just when we think a political system, a philosophy, or an attitude is true and fixed for all time, it is swept away by some revolution. Those systems (like atheistic communism) that are built on false premises simply cannot stand. Like the house built on sand, they must fall when the tide comes in. Does our Western, materialistic society seem thoroughly rationalistic, atheistic, despairing, and brutal? All the more reason to believe that the edifice is about to crumble and that everyone will soon be swept away by the supernatural, fascinated by faith, and enchanted by the romance of religion.

It is a sad diagnosis, but the Western mind is seriously sick. Like the psychotic, we can't think straight anymore—even if we want to. Like the psychotic, we have only two options: either we drift further into the nothing of nihilism and continue to commit a kind of cultural and corporate suicide, or we get better. And to turn away from the dark void means we become romantics once more. We realize we are members of a frail and finite little race, and as such we are all a little bit mad. Because we are limited in our knowledge, even the sanest of us are slightly insane. Our limitations are a kind of madness, and we can only choose to deny we are mad—and so descend into a dark spiral of total insanity—or accept we are mad and embark on a quest to regain our true and wholesome sanity.

To do this we need to engage in battle with the dark and embark on a valiant quest. We need to find the costume cupboard, dust off the broad-brimmed hat of the musketeer, practice brandishing the rapier, and fare forward to defend the honor of our beloved. I'm suggesting that, like old Don Quixote, we blow the dust off our books of chivalry, don a suit of armor, whistle for Rocinante, and ride out to joust with windmills. In other words, we need to discover once again that we have something to die for, for it is only when we have something to die for that we have something to live for.

> *We need to discover once again that we have something to die for, for it is only when we have something to die for that we have something to live for.*

The Quaint Romantic Hero

An English friend delivered a backhand slam some time ago when she said with a snooty smile, "The Americans are so quaint! They still think it is possible to be heroes." I felt chastened, but I had to admit it: some of us (and not just the

Americans) retain the romantic hero as our role model. We cheerfully concede that there is something absurd about the romantic hero. He is not a sensible sort of soul. We know that had Romeo been a practical man, he would have chosen dull friends, gone to a good school, married the Montague next door, and inherited the family business. The noble Narnian mouse Reepicheep would have stayed home to consolidate his collection of fine cheeses, and Don Quixote would not have set off as a knight in rusty armor but would have entered a rest home to play checkers and watch daytime TV.

> *Had Romeo been a practical man,*
> *he would have chosen dull friends,*
> *gone to a good school, married*
> *the Montague next door, and*
> *inherited the family business.*

But then, the romantic hero has always been a figure of fun. He is blamed not only for being romantic but for being obstinate. "You are a bombastic fool!" his sensible critics cry. "You are an absurd poseur, an amateur, and a fake!" they accuse. "You deal in generalities, broadsides, and caricatures!"

Of course, the critics are right. The romantic hero strides through life with an air of superiority. That is not because he thinks himself better than everyone else but simply because he is looking in a different direction. His nose is in the air not because he looks down on others but because he is looking up. The romantic hero marches to a different drumbeat not because he wants everyone else to march with him but because he wants them to hear that a different drumbeat and a different way of marching exist.

We admire the romantic, but we also admit that there is something dangerous about the romantic hero. We are frightened of anyone who is willing to die for his beliefs. We've seen people fly airplanes into skyscrapers. The problem there, however, is not the willingness to die for one's beliefs but the willingness to kill those who do not share those beliefs. There is all the difference between a martyr and a murderer, even if the murderer thinks he is a martyr.

A Nose by Any Other Name . . .

I confessed to my English lady friend that I am unashamed to believe that both romanticism and heroism are still possible. I brandish this belief like a white plume, which brings me to my favorite among all the romantic heroes of the world. He is the fictionalized Frenchman Cyrano de Bergerac. Cyrano is a swashbuckling poet with a monstrous nose—a character who makes more enemies than friends and who practices swordplay and wordplay at the same time, composing poems against pride and puncturing pomposity with a pun. Is there anyone in the history of the world more romantic and absurd? A tragic character with a rubber nose—more a clown than a Hamlet—takes the stage in big boots and a broad-brimmed hat to swagger over his inferiors and swoon over his lady.

With supreme confidence Cyrano ridicules his enemies

with riddles and skewers them with a song. He is the quintessential romantic hero as he mocks the hypocrite, denounces the dilettante, and woos the fair Roxanne with a rhyme. Cyrano is brave, noble, and true both in victory and defeat. In fact, it is in his defeat that his nobility is tested and proved, for it is when the brave are crushed by the ruthless and the loyal are laughed at by traitors that the romantic soul's nobility is confirmed.

Cyrano accepts rejection as the price of honesty and failure as the price of nobility. In the last act of the play by Rostand, he dies after being ambushed by an enemy. A blockhead drops a block on Cyrano's noble head, and in a magnificent climax, the hero draws his sword for the last time and duels with the shadowy figures of cowardice and corruption, duplicity and death.

In a final flamboyant gesture, Cyrano holds aloft the white plume from his broad-brimmed hat. He might just as well have pointed his magnificent nose into the air as a defiant symbol of his romantic and indomitable character. Cyrano's nose is his red badge of courage and the symbol of his nobility, but it is also the red nose of the clown and the sign of his absurdity. This is why Cyrano is the quintessential romantic hero—not only because he is intelligent, courteous, courageous, and true, but because he is absurd. He is a swashbuckling fool, a hilarious hero; a cross between d'Artagnan and Jimmy Durante. His nobility, like his nose, is both admirable and laughable.

As such, Cyrano de Bergerac is an exemplar for all who are romantics in our cynical and utilitarian age. In a world where truth is "what works for you," the fool who proposes that truth is objective will seem as laughable as Cyrano with his rubber nose. In an age where beauty is a skeletal slattern, a porno-graphic picture, or a butch biker with tattoos, the one who believes in the frail beauty of Belle or Beatrice or the Blessed Virgin is an amusing and archaic knight. In a world where the bottom line is the profit margin, one who seeks the top line of honesty and honor will seem like a ridiculous Don Quixote.

Truth is Beauty and Beauty, Truth

It is popularly thought that the romantic is simply one who has fallen in love, but the real romantic has fallen in love with something greater than a beautiful human being. He has fallen in love with beauty itself. The romantic is on a quest for the absolute; he is in love with the beloved and with beauty because they are expressions of the absolute. The romantic's real love, therefore, is the love of truth, and he finds his truth not in philosophical or theological theories but in philosophical and theological stories. A little linguistic sleight of hand will help to make my point. The word *romantic* comes from the word *romance*, which comes from the word *roman*, which is the French word for "story." (More particularly, a chivalric story written in the language of Rome.)

> *The romantic's real love, therefore, is the love of truth, and he finds his truth not in philosophical or theological theories but in philosophical and theological stories.*

I will return to that particular Roman story later, but for now the romantic, if you like, is one who not only likes stories; he believes in stories. He does not believe the stories as one believes a well-researched biography or historical account. He believes in stories as we believe in fairy tales, legends, myths, and movies—not necessarily because they are factual, but because they are true.

In other words, the romantic loves a fine romance, and by "a fine romance" I do not mean candlelit dinners, whispered words, and the mellow voice of Andy Williams singing "Moon River." A fine romance is a good story—a story, like all good stories everywhere and at every time, that reveals eternal truth within a gripping tale. We are entranced by a good story because the plot is slick and the storyteller skilled. We are captivated by a good story because it incarnates the truth. A good storyteller locks the truth so tightly into the story that you cannot get at the truth without telling the story. The romantic believes the truth in the story, but he also believes that he can make that story come true in his own life.

Consequently, when the romantic sees Cyrano de Bergerac duel with death and then gasp his last, he wipes his tears and vows in his heart that he, too, will be a noble soul and do battle with the forces of cowardice and compromise, duplicity and death. The true romantic rises up and cheers when Luke Skywalker drops a bomb into the heart of the Death Star—not because the good guys won, but because the hero took a spiritual decision to "go with the force." The romantic soul cheers because at that point he has decided (whether he knows it or not) to go with the force forever and to lead the life of the conquering hero.

The Hidden Hero

If this is the definition of the romantic, then almost all of us are romantics at heart. Simply take us into the darkened hush of the cinema or theater and all our cynicism drops away. Allow us for one moment to be entranced by the spell of the storyteller, and the Cyrano de Bergerac in each one of us comes alive. There in the darkness the child within still believes that there are such things as truth, beauty, and goodness. Even when we lapse into cynicism, doubt, and despair, the romantic in us lives—otherwise why would we be cynical and despairing?

The reason we become cynical is that we have come to believe that the ideals we thought were true are not true after all, or if they are true, they are impossible. We lapse into despair because we have lost the hope that goodness, truth, and beauty will prevail in the end. Thus, even the most despairing cynic proves that the romantic's beliefs and hopes are an indelible and universal part of the human heart. If you like, cynicism and despair exist like parasites on belief and hope. You could say that despair is the compliment the cynic pays to the romantic idealist.

*Despair is the compliment the cynic
pays to the romantic idealist.*

So the romantic, like the child within, continues to exist. The reason we dare not recognize the sleeping romantic is that we are frightened. Like the adolescent who has been wounded in love, we avoid the romantic way because we fear we may be hurt again. We assume a mask of insouciant indifference because we fear that the romantic way will expose our vulnerabilities. We affect intellectual superiority because we fear that the romantic way will lead us to absurdity, foolishness, and failure, never realizing that it is only in our absurdity and foolishness that we will discover our dignity and purpose.

The best joke is on the person who attempts to be dignified and serious. If the Lord Mayor's trousers fall down, it is far funnier than if the slave's trousers slip. The only people I can't take seriously are the people who take themselves seriously. Therefore, the person I find most ridiculous is myself, since I am constantly being made aware of how very seriously I usually take myself. I must remember that it is only at the point of absurdity, foolishness, and failure that I begin to find real meaning, wisdom, and success. It is only when we realize that we know nothing that we can begin to learn everything. It is only when we stop standing on our dignity and start stumbling over our foolishness that we begin to find wisdom. It is only when we realize that we were absurd all along that we can begin to enjoy the joke, and in laughter at ourselves we acquire real dignity.

The child at the heart of each one of us is a romantic. That romantic may be timid. He may be asleep. He may be wearing a grown-up mask of suspicion, cynicism, anger, and despair, or he may be wearing a mask of jolly indifference or stoical resignation, but still the romantic lies there, even if he is terminally ill. Those who remove their masks, take a risk, and take up the quest are the foolish but wise ones. If you are one of those, or suspect you may be, or if you know you are not but want to be, then this book may inspire and instruct you to pick up the map and go farther in the quest.

If you, on the other hand, are convinced that life is simply for pleasure or simply to be endured, then you must follow the logic to nihilism and nothing. Because you are reading this book, you should be warned that your objective, distanced approach will not be allowed to last for long. You will discover that reading this book is like being in the audience for an unusual play. This drama is designed around audience participation. You are welcome to stay in your seat, but you will eventually be invited onto the stage to play a part. No one will force you to participate, but if you do not, then eventually you will be left in your seat alone. The curtain will come down, the play will be over, the stage manager will bring the house lights down, and you will be left in the dark.

If, however, you wish to take part in the drama, you may join that huge portion of humanity who have risked their dignity and stepped out to follow the path of the hero and the romance of religion.

ALL ER NUTHIN'

The Non-Romantic Options

There's a romantic duet in the corny musical *Oklahoma!* in which Will tells his girl, Ado Annie, that for him it's "all er nuthin'." He's not going to put up with a now-and-then kind of wife. "No half-and-half romance will do!"[1]

I confess, I like Broadway musicals. I like them because the characters face life's great questions in a down-to-earth way for ordinary folk to consider. The corn might be as high as an elephant's eye, but corn is a staple food for ordinary people, and the two ordinary lovers are asking a comical question with roots that go down into the very deepest choices and questions of life. They're right. Whether we are choosing a spouse or a religion or a philosophy to guide us, we've got to make a choice. It has to be all or nothing. A half-and-half romance won't do.

The romantic is a person who believes such a choice is vital if life is to have meaning. He realizes that what he believes influences everything he thinks, says, and does. The romantic accepts with childlike wisdom that he needs something to believe in. The antiromantic believes that such an approach is sad and naive, because to believe in something means that there has to be something to believe in. In other words, there has to be such a thing as truth, and the antiromantic cynic does not believe that objective truth is possible. When you turn this inside out, however, isn't it the antiromantic who is sad and naive? He seriously believes he can go through life not believing anything, never seeing the fact that is larger than a rubber nose on his face—to believe belief is impossible is, in fact, to believe in something. Compared to such self-deception, the romantic is a cold, hard realist.

Daydream Believer

In the face of cynicism, doubt, and despair, the romantic is an unashamed believer. He believes in something bigger, older, and more eternal than his own small life. He believes that truth, beauty, and love are real and that life is not worth living unless it is a quest to find and hold these elusive and eternal treasures. The true romantic is not naive. He does not believe that the quest to find truth, beauty, goodness, and love is easy. He accepts that the quest is enigmatic, complex, and strange. He knows that the quest is so dangerous that his very life may be required. The romantic is one who has either set out on that ancient and beautiful quest or, at least, has decided to seek the courage to begin.

The unromantic person, on the other hand, is an unbeliever. He does not believe there is anything bigger, older, and more eternal than his own life. He believes truth, beauty, goodness, and love are figments of the imagination—at best, useful and delightful fictions. The purest antiromantic is the logical positivist. He is the hardheaded and hard-hearted fellow who refuses to accept any form of knowledge that cannot be verified by the physical senses. I don't believe I have ever met a purely consistent logical positivist. There aren't many about anymore because science has shown how rubbery the physical world really is. It turns out that matter is only an arrangement of energy, and when it is all boiled down we realize that the perceptions of the senses may simply be no more than chemical reactions in the brain. Did I really see, touch, taste, hear, or smell something, or were those sensations simply a sequence of electrical reactions within my neurological systems?

As a result, the poor old logical positivist cannot even rely on his physical senses to determine truth and must conclude that the physical world is nothing but a whirl of energy and some sort of cranial chemical combustion. The delicious irony of this is that the one who believes only in physically observable phenomena must draw the conclusion that there is no such thing as physically observable phenomena. For the religious romantic, who thinks this physical world is passing away, this truth is an exciting confirmation of what he has always believed. For the logical positivist it must be positively disturbing. What he thought was the only reality proves to be nothing but a fizz pop in his brain. If a logical positivist continues to preach his gospel—that there is nothing but the physical world—then he ends up with nothing. It must be for him a very confusing and irrational state of mind, but it illustrates the sad but comical truth that the logical positivist has ended up being neither logical nor positive.

> *The logical positivist has ended up
> being neither logical nor positive.*

Snap, Crackle, Pop—the Cosmos

This scientific uncertainty has thrown us into a kind of relativism where no one believes that any kind of truth is possible at all, and the only thing we can hope for is mutual tolerance because everything (including ourselves) is at best a matter of opinion, or at worst a figment of our imagination. If all our physical sensations are merely electrochemical reactions in the brain, then the whole sad, hilarious, and glorious world is no more than a fizzle and a pop in my head. Alice's Wonderland was the result of a dream—maybe the whole cosmos is too.

This is the end of logical positivism, and it is the end of any philosophy that excludes the supernatural in favor of the merely natural. The logical positivist believes only in the physical world. The supernaturalist believes in that world, but he also believes in another, invisible world. As a result, the supernaturalist embraces both the visible and invisible worlds. He has both. On the other hand, when the physical world known by sensation proves to be ephemeral, the logical positivist, because he does not admit the possibility of the supernatural, ends up losing the natural as well. The options really are all-or-nothing. If we choose all—both visible and invisible—we have chosen all of life, love, mystery, and meaning. If we choose nothing, then that is what we get, for we realize very sadly that if we have chosen just the natural world, in the end it doesn't last and there is simply death. Nothing. Nada. Zilch. "The unimaginable zero summer."[2]

Stoics or Epicureans All

The honest and thoughtful unbeliever accepts the inevitable zero. He accepts the "dark dark dark. They all go into the dark,"[3] and responds in one of two ways. He is either cheerful or austere. The cheerful ones we call Epicureans because, whether they know it or not, they follow the ancient and practical school of philosophy that seeks to enjoy life while it lasts. The manner in which Epicureans enjoy life varies enormously. Epicureans might be riotous party animals or refined patricians. They might like opera and canapés or orgies and cans of beer. They might enjoy balls or ball games, hors d'oeuvres or hot dogs; they might be philanderers or philosophers, aesthetes or ascetics, gluttons or connoisseurs. In a way it doesn't matter because their final conclusion is the same: life is to be enjoyed while it lasts, because only one thing is sure—it will not last.

This same sobering truth is faced differently by the other category of nonromantics. Those who face their ultimate and certain destruction in an austere way we call Stoics because, whether they know it or not, they follow that other ancient and practical school of philosophy that seeks a good life, not through debauchery, but through duty. A Stoic believes the suffering of life should be avoided through discipline and noble behavior. Stoics follow their creed in all sorts of practical ways. They might give their lives in heroic good works for the sake of others. They might live to make the world a better place. They might discipline their appetites and control their desires, knowing that indulgence leads to excess and excess leads to suffering. The Stoic might be generous, kind, noble, and good, but beneath it all runs the echo of despair and the gnawing knowledge that Mr. Death will come knocking.

There are multitudes of different ways to be either a Stoic or an Epicurean, but while there are many paths to death, there is only one way to die, and it is that great, unavoidable truth that eventually consigns both the cheerful Epicurean and the austere Stoic to the same category. Both believe that there is nothing after this life. In the end, how they cope with this truth is irrelevant. In the end, both the cheerful Epicurean and the austere Stoic are wearing masks. Like the Greek masks for tragedy and comedy, one is sad and one is happy, but beneath both masks they are neither cheerful nor austere but despairing.

If death will devour us, then what is there really worth living for? And if there is nothing worth living for, why go on living? Underneath both the Epicurean and the Stoic response is a far more realistic philosophical category: nihilism. The nihilist is simply an Epicurean or a Stoic who has done his homework, thought things through, and realized that death (if death is final) renders irrelevant all attempts to find truth, beauty, and goodness. Cynicism and despair are simply the emotions that accompany nihilism.

> *The nihilist is simply an Epicurean or a Stoic who has done his homework.*

The Stoic and the Epicurean seem to be very practical and realistic. The romantic, on the other hand, looks increasingly like an unrealistic fool. In the face of death, he holds to his belief with a touching bravado. Like Cyrano, he duels with death to the bitter end. Like the valiant Narnian mouse Reepicheep, he jousts with giants. Even though he faces defeat, the romantic believes that he will overcome. For the romantic every defeat is only a setback. He may lose battle after battle, but he never entertains the idea that he will lose the war. This romance seems dead in our modern life. We have been taught to believe nothing, to doubt everything, and to take no one's word for it. We have been taught to be cynical of the romantic, to debunk the idealist, to doubt the believer, and to discredit the zealot.

The Way of Adventure

Yet within every human heart there is still a yearning. We know that the Epicurean way is not true. We know that it ends in either a lonely stone gutter or a lonely ivory tower. We also know that the Stoic way leads only to a noble despair and that the final stoical act is suicide. So we turn again, longing for something more. The romantic strain in every human soul cannot be quenched by cynicism and despair any more than a candle can be quenched by the darkness.

The romantic way is an adventure with both great risks and great gains. On the other hand, to endure life as a cynic is at best jaded and dull, and at worst bitter and despairing. It is a dead-end street. Think of it like this: We all stand on the deck of a sinking ship. The Epicurean enjoys a five-course meal and drinks a cocktail and dances while the ship goes down. The Stoic gives up his lifejacket and stands on the bridge in silent dignity, awaiting the deluge. But the romantic spots a distant light, decides it is a lifeboat, then jumps in to either swim for safety or die in the attempt.

THE *MATRIX* AND MY MICKEY MOUSE LUNCH BOX

The Quest for Something More

I have already mentioned the moment in fifth grade when, on a big yellow school bus, the future opened and I realized what I was not going to do. Four years before this, at the beginning of first grade, the yellow school bus became my transportation not into school, but into another world. Because of the long ride to school each day, I had considerable time for the contemplation of metaphysical problems. A particular conundrum was caused by my Mickey Mouse lunch box. I remember very clearly that my lunch box was painted to look like a big yellow school bus, just like the very one I was sitting in.

On the outside of the lunch box were printed various Disney characters cheerfully riding off to school. On this happy lunch box was a most disturbing detail. At the door, waiting to board this Disneyfied school bus, stood Mickey Mouse himself. Mickey was waving with innocent enthusiasm, but the intriguing and somewhat sinister thing about Mickey is that he was holding a yellow school bus lunch box that was identical to mine.

On the way to first grade, this made me think. If I had a lunch box with Mickey Mouse on it, and if Mickey held an identical lunch box, did Mickey's lunch box have another Mickey Mouse holding another identical lunch box? I looked closely and sure enough, there on Mickey's little lunch box was another, minute Mickey clutching another lunch box just like mine.

Now, what made my six-year-old head spin was the question, did that tiny Mickey also have a lunch box on which there was yet another happy Mickey with an even tinier lunch box with yet another minute Mickey happily going off to school on a yellow bus? Logic demanded there be ever more and ever more minute Mickeys on lunch box after lunch box, ad infinitum. Was the everlasting succession of tiny Mickeys and lunch boxes there even though I could not see them?

There seemed to be worlds within worlds within worlds. *Is the cosmos like this?* I wondered. Were there more worlds locked inside this one, with even more locked in each one of them, on and on forever? Was the cosmos one big onion or a Russian doll, with layer upon layer of reality—each one lying inside the next, each one more beautiful and intense than the one before? Was my yellow school bus the transportation to some inner realm of wonder? Did I hold in the form of my Mickey Mouse lunch box a metaphor of eternity? Was this ordinary container for peanut butter sandwiches, a cookie, an apple, and a thermos of juice a pointer to other worlds? Was my Mickey Mouse lunch box not just an advertisement for Disneyland but an advertisement for Wonderland and Neverland? Did I hold in my hands a magical transporter to another dimension? Were there dragons, elves, wizards, and fairy godmothers inside? What if I opened it and found not a sandwich but a witch? What if that sandwich contained not Peter Pan peanut butter but Peter Pan himself?

> *Did I hold in the form of my*
> *Mickey Mouse lunch box a*
> *metaphor of eternity?*

Unfortunately my first grade teacher did not discuss these matters in class. If she had the answers, she wasn't telling. She seemed more concerned with tiresome matters like keeping order, singing "The Farmer in the Dell," and teaching us to spell. Nevertheless, the world of childhood is not lacking in similarly fascinating riddles. Indeed, I suspect far more contemplation of metaphysical problems takes place in the minds of six-year-olds than sixty-year-olds. Children are curious. They are fascinated by other worlds, the spiritual dimension, and life after death. One of the reasons they like fairy tales is that through them they can play with their exciting playmates called good and evil, magic and mystery, time and eternity, destiny and death.

Myth, Metaphysics, and *The Matrix*

The possibility of another unseen world running parallel to this one is the complex premise of the stylish movie *The Matrix*. The hero, "Neo" Anderson, is locked in a boring, artificial world as an office drone when he hears the call to adventure. He is told that his "real" world is, in fact, a computerized artifice. The really real world, he is told, exists on a different plane altogether. He is challenged to go through the looking glass to the real world, then return to do battle in the artificial world for all that is beautiful, true, and real. Neo's wake-up call makes him aware of the existence of the other world, and his quest is to give up everything for reality.

The modern fairy tale of *The Matrix* is as old as Jason's quest for the Golden Fleece and Parsifal's search for the Holy Grail. In the stories of every age, the hero is a romantic character who is shaken from the slumber of his ordinary world and called to embark on a heroic quest. As I studied Mickey Mouse on my lunch box and wondered if there was more, so the hero puzzles over the mundane details of ordinary life and tries to figure out the riddle. He traces in his ordinary world the signs of a larger, better life and the pattern of mystery and meaning that is far more tremendous than he could ever have imagined.

The mythologist Joseph Campbell studied the stories of

cultures around the world and discovered that a pattern runs through them all. All the great stories are stories of romantic heroes. Legends, myths, folklore, and fairy tales enchant us with the accounts of ordinary men and women who hear a call to adventure and leave everything to find some great treasure.

The meaning of life is to ask a question, and the question is, what is the meaning of life?

Their calling disturbs their peace. It upsets their comfortable little worlds. It whispers to them that their ordinary worlds are simply portals into other realms. The call is an enchantment that reminds them that there is more, yet more, and that their ordinary worlds are cramped, limited, narrow, and dark. At first the hero refuses the call because he feels inadequate, frightened, confused, or simply lazy. Then he meets a mentor—some wise older person who affirms the validity of his call and encourages him to embark on the adventure. Once on the roller coaster of his adventure, the hero encounters enemies and allies. He learns how to be a hero—not by sitting at home thinking about it, but by taking a risk and setting out on the quest.

The hero embarks on a quest because he has asked a question. In fact, he has decided that the meaning of life is to ask a question, and the question is, what is the meaning of life? Gradually, it dawns on the hero that the answer is not simply a formula or a phrase. It is not even a dictum or a doctrine. It is more than rules and regulations and rubrics. The answer to the question is to go on a quest.

Hollywood and the Holy Wood

In ancient times heroic stories were told by wealthy and powerful wizards who lived on holy mountains or in sacred groves. Today heroic stories are told by wealthy and powerful wizards who live not in a holy wood, but in Hollywood. In ancient times the people sat in the dark around the flickering campfire to hear the mysterious adventures of the hero. Today we sit in the darkened cinema around the flickering lights of the film projector to share in the same forms of elemental heroic drama. Aristotle understood the mysterious workings of drama. He knew how we bond with the mythic hero. The ancient Greeks, enthralled by the drama of gods and men, were enchanted by the same principles that captivate us when we sit with a box of popcorn to yield ourselves to the magic of the latest blockbuster.

> *Today heroic stories are told by wealthy and powerful wizards who live not in a holy wood, but in Hollywood.*

The scriptwriters, directors, and actors all conspire to get us to love the hero. The hero must always be an ordinary person, because it is from the ordinary that we step into the extraordinary, and we step from the ordinary into the extraordinary in order to see that the extraordinary has been hidden in the ordinary all the time—just as it was in the mysterious matrix of my Mickey Mouse lunch box.

As the hero goes on his quest, he invariably stumbles and falls, and as he falls, we fall with him, and as we fall with him, we fall in love with him. That is to say, we identify with him. We share his problems. He becomes our brother and our friend. When he makes a decision, we make the decision with him until, at last, we are drawn by the drama into our own personal choices between good and evil. As we do, a bond between us is forged, and it is like the bond of love. We are united with the hero in a most mysterious and mystical way. We have become brothers in arms, or you could say, we have become brothers in charms.

For the story charms us. It enchants us. It casts a spell that transforms our way of seeing this world. Long ago, the stories were told by the wizards and magicians because everyone knew the magical effect of the heroic tale was a part of some deep magic from before the dawn of time. So the stories, myths, and movies enchant us like a fine romance. The reason falling in love is so intoxicating and dangerous is that we are falling, and when we are falling, we are out of control—and we are out of control because we are out of ourselves.

When we fall in love, we come to believe in someone and something greater than ourselves. Suddenly we have something else to live for, and life takes on a new dimension of reality. This is why we call these stories "make-believe"—because they make us believe. The hero starts to believe when he asks his question and embarks on his quest. He moves outside himself and comes to believe in something greater than himself. In that respect, every heroic story is a romance. And the earliest form of the romance was not really a sentimental love story but an adventure story of knights saving fair maidens from fearsome dragons. The earliest romances were tales of bravery, courage, and a holy quest.

The Religious Romantic

This is what the romance of religion is all about—it is about embarking on a quest to find the pearl of great price, the secret treasure hidden in the field, the lost coin, the lost sheep, or the lost child. To go on this adventure is to step into another dimension, not only in the next life but in this life here and now. To go on this quest demands that we step out of our ordinary world into the world of adventure. To do this we must first catch the glimpse of the truth that there is another world to step into, then hear the call to step out of one world and into another.

> *This is what the romance of religion is all about—it is about embarking on a quest to find the pearl of great price, the secret treasure hidden in the field, the lost coin, the lost sheep, or the lost child.*

The multitude of fantasy movies, stories, and fairy tales that tell stories of parallel worlds are only pointers to the fact that there really is an alternative to the desperately dull and deadly lives most of us lead. The reason the writers of the fantasy tales have the hero go to the other world through a mask, a mirror, a whirlwind, a wardrobe, or a rabbit hole is because it is through the ordinary things of life that we connect with this other world. The connecting point is not through an esoteric or ecstatic experience but through the portal of an everyday and ordinary occurrence.

The call might come to us at any time—through some great trauma or joy, or through the most ordinary and unexceptional event. The insight comes through a new way of seeing. Missouri is famously known as the Show Me State, and the man from Missouri is the classic skeptic. The problem with a skeptic is that he is antiseptic. Antiseptic kills bacteria, but it also kills beer, for beer requires bacteria. Similarly, life requires risk, and the skeptic, like the antiseptic, kills everything he touches. The Man from Missouri says, "Show me," but refuses to look. He says, "Seeing is believing," but refuses to open his eyes.

The requirement for stepping through the whirlwind, the wardrobe, the mask, or the mirror into another world is the ability, first of all, to find the mask or the mirror, the wardrobe, the trapdoor, to find the magic red pill that transports you from the merely physical to the metaphysical. To discover this requires an understanding of the mechanics of metaphysics, and like the preparation for any adventure, this takes a dash of curiosity, a splash of study, and a gasp of sudden, unexpected enlightenment.

OF WHIRLWINDS, WORDS, AND OTHER WORLDS

The Grammar of Romance

The materialist critics of religion sneer, "I hear all this talk of heroes and quests, but your castles are nothing but castles in the air. It is nothing but a dream of the big grand-daddy in the sky who gives you what you want if you're good little boys and girls! It is all child's play. It is fairy-tale foolish-ness! Why don't you people get real?" This not only shows how little the materialist understands religion; it also shows how little he understands fairy tales, how little he under-stands children, and how little he understands reality.

The religious romantic replies to the critic, "Of course

33

religion is like a fairy tale! Of course it is child's play. That's the whole point! We like child's play. In fact, we believe the saying that 'unless you become as a little child, you cannot enter this magical kingdom.'[1] Don't you see that the whole point of fairy tales, fantasy films, and fantastic fiction is to teach us about reality? You ask us to 'get real.' Reality is precisely what we are getting." The religious romantic continues, "We don't just tell fairy tales. We don't just believe fairy tales. We live them. Don't you see that our religion is the way we go on the great quest? This is the way we ride out to tilt at windmills, slay the dragon, and rescue the fair maiden. It is through our religion that we kill the wicked witch, slay the dragon, figure out the riddle, and find our way home, and it is through this that we meet with true reality. Don't you see? Don't you see?"

> *"Of course religion is like a fairy tale! Of course it is child's play. That's the whole point!"*

This is exactly what the materialist cannot do: he cannot see. What he cannot see is the invisible, yet the invisible is exactly what he must learn to see. The materialist cannot understand what on earth the religious romantic is talking about because what the religious romantic is talking about is something that is not on the earth. He is talking about something that is in heaven. Now, *heaven* is a heavenly word, and it is also a heavy word. It carries a lot of weight. There is more to it than meets the ear, and to explain what I mean by the word *heaven*, I would like to take a side trip into the meaning of words themselves.

You may find this little excursion into the magical realm of language to be confusing or complex. That is part of the adventure. Gather your courage and cleverness and attempt to solve the riddle. Here we go.

The Mechanics of Metaphysics

There once was a gentle Englishman who lived in a large house in the country beside a river that flowed down to a meadow on which stood a beautiful cathedral. The man helped the poor people in the village and ministered to the sick. He was a country parson, so he went to church to pray. He was also a poet and a prophet and a priest, and his name was George Herbert.

Herbert was one of a group of poets the critics call the "metaphysical poets." They are given that name because they wrote paradoxical and pure poems about mysterious subjects. In their own way they were authors of fairy tales. They were fantasy poets, for they wrote not of elves but angels; not of Neverland but the Everland of eternity. To discuss such extraordinary subjects, they used very ordinary objects. George Herbert wrote about a collar, a meal, a path, a friend, and as he did, he referred to a spiritual attachment, a mystical meal, a mysterious journey, and an invisible friend. The metaphysical poets were intellectual and witty. They liked to play with words and other worlds.

This is really why George Herbert was a metaphysical: *meta* means "to change" or magically transform, and he and his friends used language to magically change their readers' perceptions, and as they changed their perceptions they changed *them*. It was, if you like, metaphysical metamorphosis through metaphors. The metaphysical poets leapfrogged from ordinary things to extraordinary things with a dash of wit and a flash of insight. In fact, that is what every poet does. He constantly reads extraordinary realities into the ordinary world. A rose, for the poet, is not just a rose but his lover. A tree is not a tree but a key that locks together earth and sky. A bee is not just a bee but a miniature miner of nectar, a minute manufacturer of honey. For the poet, the bee creates the food of angels and so becomes a winged messenger for the winged messengers of God.

To think is to make connections, and to make unusual connections is the wildest and most wonderful kind of thinking. Anyone can see the connection between a black dog and his collar; some people might see a dog collar and see a priest; but only a poet sees that every priest is a black dog in a white collar. Poets are gymnasts. They use language as a trampoline, not just to do backflips, but to ascend higher into the sky than the rest of us. As they do their verbal barrel rolls, they are simply doing us the service of showing us what all of us do whenever we use language at all.

When I use a word, I make a connection between a concrete object and an abstract subject. In other words, I connect the thing I can see with the idea I cannot see. If my beloved is named Lucy, then when I say, "Lucy," I connect my beloved not only with my mental image of my beloved but with Love itself, and when I say, "love," I think not only of my beloved's name but of her face, her hair, her smile, the way she smacks a tennis ball, the way she shrieks with laughter, sobs in grief, and burns the dinner. Whenever we use any word in any way, we are being metaphorical and metaphysical, because words help us transcend the merely physical.

Words take us into the realm of ideas, and the realm of ideas is next door to the realm of ideals. "Ideals" in this context are "universals," or what the philosopher Plato called "forms." Ideals, or forms, are those ideas that are greater than our own individual ideas and that last forever. If the philosophers are right, then humans have this gift called language that links the ordinary things in our lives and our ordinary ideas to what is extraordinary and eternal, and we forget what a startling gift it is. It is language that puts us among the angels rather than the apes. Animals grunt. Humans make poems. A gorilla may be taught sign language, but he will never write a sonnet.

Of Words and Other Worlds

Humans have words that connect us with the eternal because humans have souls that are eternal. That is why poets play with words—because they take us to other worlds. As the poet transports us to another realm, so also the fantasy writer tells stories that take us to other worlds. The cynic says, "Wait a moment! These other worlds are only within your imagination!" He is correct. How else but through our imaginations would we be able to go to other worlds? His observation that these worlds exist in our imagination is very dull. It is like seeing a person who has just walked from Tibet to Timbuktu and remarking, "All this talk of a great journey! All you have done is walk on your ordinary two legs! There is not much in that!" But as legs are for walking, so imagination is for going to other worlds, and language is our mode of travel.

> *As legs are for walking, so imagination is for going to other worlds, and language is our mode of travel.*

Some people who study the ancient languages blame the ancient peoples for being primitive because their languages have a small vocabulary and are imprecise. They suppose that the ancient language with its tiny vocabulary has progressed to the language we now have with a huge vocabulary. But they have it exactly back to front. What has really happened is that our language has decayed. It is a sign of our mental and spiritual dullness that we need more words, not fewer. It is a sign of our ancestors' mental sophistication that they communicated very well with fewer words. We blame them for being stupid because they had fewer words, when in fact we are stupid for needing so many words.

An example is the Hebrew word *ruach*. This word means "breath," but for the Hebrews it meant not only the breath going in and out of a human set of lungs. It was also the bellowing wind of a terrible storm, the gentle breeze in the trees, and the breath of God, puffing into the lungs of the man he had just formed out of the clay of the earth. It was Life. It was the Lord of Life. It was the Holy Spirit—the breath and life of God himself.

Heaven is another word that is heavy with meaning. The literalist thinks heaven is a place beyond the clouds with angels playing harps and where everyone is happy forever and ever. However, heaven is more than cotton-candy clouds and chubby cherubs. Heaven is also the realm above the earth. It is the sky, and the sky stands for all that is real but spiritual. The *heavens* are over the earth, but they also come down and touch the earth. The *kingdom of heaven* is therefore that realm that is above and beyond this realm. It is not only the realm of the ethereal; it is the realm of the real.

Our ancestors were metaphorical and metaphysical in their very way of thinking and viewing the world. For them the whole world was charged with the grandeur of God. The words they used, with their multiplicity of meanings, showed an abundance, not a poverty, of thought. In their use of language, they saw and knew what the poets saw and knew without having to be poets. What they knew was that a word connected their visible world with the invisible world, and what they saw was the invisible world blazing quietly within the visible world. Language is therefore the bridge between all things seen and unseen. It is the link between two types of reality: one that they sensed and one that was sensational. The words connected the lower reality with the higher reality.

This is how the religious romantic sees the world. Every physical thing is loaded with the whole cosmos. The poet sees eternity in a grain of sand.[2] For him, therefore, each word is full of mystical and magnificent meaning. If you like, every word is a world, and every word and every world is a whirlwind that transports him to the other country. This is why the romantic religious person values words. This is why the heroes in the fairy tales have to learn the words of a potent spell, solve a riddle, memorize a code, compose a poem, or recite a magic incantation.

There is more. If the words connected visible things with the invisible, then the ancients concluded that the reverse was also true. It is easy to imagine that primitive people saw physical things and made up a word for them. They decided that the reverse is true. The visible, physical world was not first, but the word was first. Dog was not there and God said, "Dog." God said, "Dog," and dog was there. Thus the ancients understood that the world came from a word through the whirlwind, and they derived the formula that there was, therefore, one Word from which came all words and all worlds. So they said, "In the beginning was the Word, and through the Word all things live and move and have their being."[3] This is what I mean by the mechanics of metaphysics: the simple use of words themselves connects us with the Word beyond all words, and with the other worlds within the words, and other worlds with us.

The ancients understood that the world came from a word through the whirlwind, and they derived the formula that there was, therefore, one Word from which came all words and all worlds.

The Word from which all words are derived, and on which all words depend, is only another way of talking about an ultimate reality—the reality that the romantic religious person attempts to explore. He believes that other reality is there and is not surprised to discover that the greatest of the old philosophers agree. They thought there was another realm for some very good reasons. They taught that beneath and beyond each physical thing was its "substance." This "substance" was the essence of the thing: its reality, the part of it that could not change or decay. If they saw a table, they thought that the table was only a table because it was an expression of the one great Table in which all tables root their existence. If this sounds ephemeral and airy-fairy, it is good to be reminded that the people who believed in this invisible, eternal realm were called "realists."

They were called realists because they believed not only in the possibility of reality but the necessity of reality. They believed that the physical realm (which dies and decays and turns to dust) could not possibly be real, because it was temporal. It turned to dust in time. It was not eternal. Because the physical realm was forever disintegrating, they concluded that its seeming solidity was an illusion. Therefore, for physical things to be real at all, they had to depend on a greater reality, and that greater reality had to be one that was greater than we could sense with our physical senses, because our physical senses can only perceive that which is passing away.

The invisible realm, on the other hand, while seeming less real, suddenly seems the only reality that is left. The invisible realm of reality—the world of the Word—is the foundation for all reality, and not accepting this is not a failure of imagination but a failure of reason. To believe that the physical world was the real world was to believe something that was obviously untrue. How could that which dies and decays and disintegrates to dust be the real world? How can that which is perceived with our senses be truly real when our senses are only chemical fizz pops in our brain? How can that seemingly solid stone be real when the scientist himself tells me it is no more than a buzz of energy and invisible particles?

To insist that the physical is the only real world is to fall for an illusion far more illusory than any fairy tale. Instead, if the modern physicists and ancient sages are right, the real world is not the one you see, but the one you don't see, and the way to get real is to open your eyes and see what is invisible.

Either the Ethereal
or the Real

The Illusions of Reality

In one of his science-fiction books, C. S. Lewis portrays an angelic being who moves through a solid brick wall, and when the hero asks if this ethereal being is real, he is challenged about the nature of reality. The angel passed through the brick wall, but what if it was the brick wall that passed through the angel? Lewis points out that this is all a matter of one's perspective and perception. If you saw a man step through an opaque bank of fog, and you did not know that the fog was really a wall of mist, you might think that the man was a ghost or a spirit. He had, after all, according to your perception, stepped through what seemed to be a solid wall. Of course, you would have it the wrong way around. The man stepped through the wall of fog not because he was insubstantial, but because the fog was.[1]

It has become clear that when I have been talking about fairyland and going to other worlds, I have been referring to our intercourse with the spiritual realm. To use the phrase *spiritual realm* is, in itself, misleading because by *spiritual* most people mean "ethereal," and by *ethereal* they mean "made up of ether," and ether is a gas; so what people usually mean is that when you speak of the "ethereal" you are simply gassing. In other words, you are full of hot air.

The word *spiritual* also makes them think of angels, whom they conceive either as a kind of fairy godmother or as plump, pink-bottomed cherubs or as effeminate, handsome youths with wings. Or when they think of spiritual beings, they think of ghosts—wispy illusions of smoke and shadows that disappear as soon as you say, "Boo!" When all is said and done, *spiritual* for most people means gaseous, ephemeral, nonphysical, and therefore unreal, or at least less real than all that is seemingly solid and physical.

However, this is exactly the opposite of what I think when I hear the word *spiritual*. I think the spiritual beings, like the man stepping through the fog, are more real than what we consider physical, not less real, and that the things we consider solid and physical and "real" are rather slippery and ephemeral, impermanent and insubstantial. Happily, modern physics seems to be coming around to the conclusions that ancient religion arrived at thousands of years ago.

In all sorts of ways we are learning that what we thought was solid and real is insubstantial, and what we thought was spiritual, ethereal, and unreal is the most reliable form of reality. Modern physics is now more like metaphysics because the modern physicist has shown us that what we thought was solid matter is not so solid after all. It is a tissue of energy and invisible particles bound together no one knows how. Nevertheless, our perception of reality is very convincing, and it is easy to believe that it is the only form of reality. It is not hard to imagine how one might believe a convincing illusion to be the only reality there is.

Plato at the Movies

If you go to the movie theater, you see something that seems very real. You hear the hero laugh and you see the villain sneer. The illusion is so powerful that it can make you gasp with fear, howl with laughter, and weep with poignant grief. For a few hours you are transported to a world of adventure, and the darkness of the theater allows the illusion to seem totally and utterly real. But then the credits roll, the lights come up, and you remember that it was all a temporary world created with the amazing alchemy of modern technology. In fact, the whole wonderful world was nothing but a magical mixture of music and machinery, lenses and light, and when it is reduced further, you realize that it was all a concoction of digital images and digital sound, and even these things were no more than electronic impulses chugging through a very smart machine. The illusion of the cinema is, therefore, one complex illusion piled on top of many others.

Now imagine for a moment that a person was born in

the movie theater and never went outside the movie theater. Ever. In fact, he was chained to his seat in the darkened theater and force-fed nothing but a watery gruel. He would, of course, perceive the cinematic illusion as the real world. If you went into that cinema and turned on the lights and said, "You know, all that you have seen here is merely a picture of the real world," he would not believe you. Indeed, the more you insisted and the more you cajoled and the more you tried to explain the real world outside, the more he would find your fairy tale a ridiculous fabrication. Indeed, he would find it not only ridiculous but dangerous.

> *The more you insisted and the more you cajoled and the more you tried to explain the real world outside, the more he would find your fairy tale a ridiculous fabrication.*

Let us imagine that you said to the man chained in the movie house, "The real world is like that world, but the people are not big, flat images up on a screen; they are smaller, but although they are smaller they are not less important. In fact, they are three-dimensional. They are real, and because they are real, the images you have been looking at are only worth something because of their relationship to the real people outside."

He would say, "What is 'three-dimensional'?"

You would reply, "You can walk around them. You can touch them. They are not flat. They are round."

He would say, "What is 'round'?"

And if you said, "You can eat the food. Some of it tastes good. The root beer and the roast beef are delicious. Some of it tastes bad. The red beets are bitter and the broccoli tastes bad."

He would say, "What is 'tastes'?"

And when you stopped frowning in frustration and said, "But you can smell things there. The roses you see smell beautifully sweet and the wet dogs smell like sweaty socks."

He would reply, "What is 'smell'?"

Because he had spent all his life looking at movies, he would not have the mental equipment to even begin to conceive of taste and touch and smell and what "three-dimensional" means. Locked in the cinema his whole life, he would laugh at such things. He would scorn you if you tried to convince him that another world existed, which was like the world you saw but was not less real but more real. He would consider you to be a dreamer, a fool, and a dangerous lunatic. Furthermore, if he lived in the cinema with a whole little tribe of like-minded cinema people, he would feel secure that he and his fellow movie people were right and you were wrong.

So it is with the materialist. He is trapped in his little one-dimensional movie house with his materialist friends and cannot see any farther. The saddest thing about it is that he thinks himself terribly clever for not being taken in. He imagines himself to be part of an elite group of people who have "seen through all that nonsense." In reality, he has not seen through it. He has not seen it at all. He is a human being and yet he is oblivious to the one element that makes him human: the capacity to be in touch with the spiritual realm. It is true that he is part of a small group, for the whole of the rest of humanity down through the ages have had enough sense and enough humanity to believe in the spiritual realm. All human beings, from animists and Amish and Anglicans to Methodists and Mormons and Muslims, from Buddhists to Baptists, and from pagans and Presbyterians to Catholics and Quakers and all the rest, have known that there is more to life than meets the eye, and what meets the eye is rarely what it seems.

> *He is a human being and yet he is oblivious to the one element that makes him human: the capacity to be in touch with the spiritual realm.*

The Heart of the Matter

The problem the materialist has is not that he is skeptical, but that he is not skeptical enough. He takes matter for granted and doesn't examine it as critically as he might. To understand this we have to stop for a moment and consider matter itself. Our eyes tell us that a brick is square and red and hard, and our foot tells us the same, and the nerve endings in our feet and the nerve centers in our brains tell us that the brick is very hard when we decide to kick it. All of this convinces us that the physical things we see, hear, taste, touch, and smell are real. They are real, but modern physics tells us that their reality is far stranger than we thought. It turns out that the physical things of our world are not really very solid at all.

Everything we perceive as solid is, in reality, no more than particles of this and particles of that held together by energy. These particles and energy come together to present us with what seems to be solid matter.

All of this science is very interesting to the spiritually minded mystic. It matches what he thought all along: that the physical world was not quite as substantial as his senses led him to believe. Furthermore, he is interested to learn that the energy that holds the physical world together is the same energy as light, or as one physicist, David Bohm, has said, "Matter, as it were, is condensed or frozen light,"[2] and that Einstein decided that all matter could be reduced to photons—little particles of light. If that is so, then what we call *physical* is not so very different from what we think of as spiritual after all. In the thirteenth century, Thomas Aquinas thought angels were creatures of light, so it is possible that the physical world and the spiritual world are both composed of light; it's just that they are simply composed of light in different ways, rather like rock music and the music of Rachmaninoff are both composed of sound, but in very different ways.

Why this is so hard for the materialist to accept is beyond me. After all, he himself believes in a wonderful, mysterious, invisible world, for he tells me there is a whole range of forms of light that are invisible to me, and a whole range of fields of energy that are constantly active and yet invisible to me. He tells me about radio waves and microwaves and X-rays and gamma rays, and I learn that all the forms of energy can be changed into the other forms, and that at the heart of them all they can be called *light*. And then he says that light can be trapped in material form, as when the sunlight enters a plant through photosynthesis and becomes wood.

Then he tells me that light is very mysterious and it behaves as both a particle and a wave at the same time, and that this is a deep mystery even he cannot understand or explain. In this dialogue I must accept everything he tells me about his invisible world, the mysterious powers he believes in, and the seemingly contradictory and irrational behaviors of these invisible powers. I am happy to do so, for I already believed in such things from the fairy tales and from the religions of humanity. He speaks to me of invisible particles that have unpredictable personalities and behaviors, and I can't understand why he disbelieves in angels and demons. While I accept with delight all the wonderful tales he tells me about his invisible beings and mysterious realms of power, I am sad that he scorns my own account of similar encounters.

Perception, Prophecy, and Poetry

The scientist requires curiosity and belief in the experiences of others who have gone before him to explore the exciting realm of the unknown. In that respect he is no different from the religious romantic. Both require the open mind and open heart of the child and the poet. The materialist has to accept that there may be more to the nature of reality than he first thought. He has to tremble with the awareness that perhaps, after all, there is something to tremble about, because if there is more to the nature of reality than he first thought, then there is more to himself than he first thought, and if there is more to himself than he first thought, then there may be more to his future than he first thought. The mechanics of metaphysics demand not a run from reality but a run toward reality. The reality is a deeper mystery than one can imagine, and to experience it requires the tools and tackle of religion, for religion is the way humanity has explored this other realm.

One of the reasons most modern religion is considered dull and boring is because it *is* dull and boring. Modern religious people have forgotten that religion is not about being good but about being religious. In other words, religion is about an encounter with the other world. It is about reaching for reality. Religious leaders are full of politeness. They have become charming, but they have forgotten how to charm. They have forgotten how to enchant, how to weave a spell, how to delight, and how to enlighten. This is done by making surprising connections, and this is the heart of the poetic art and is, therefore, the work of the poetic heart.

> *Religion is about an encounter*
> *with the other world. It is*
> *about reaching for reality.*

It is the work of the poet and the priest to wrest new meanings from words and to make new connections that break open our hearts so the light can get in. This process is a kind of enchantment. It is like learning and casting spells. It is using words to work a kind of magic, and this work is not only poetical, it is prophetical; and if the poet is a prophet, he is also a preacher and a priest.

Poetry is the heart of religion, and when the poetical is lost, religion has lost its heart. That is to say, it has lost its romance. The lifeblood, the beating passion of religion, has gone. Instead of poetry and prophecy, we are left with pedestrian prose and pious platitudes. Religion has become not the realm of the romantic but a list of regulations and rules, doctrines and dictums, prohibitions and polite behavior. In other words, modern religion has become merely physical rather than metaphysical. It has become concerned with making this world a better place and has forgotten the next world altogether. In other words, modern religion has ceased to be a religion at all. It has become a set of table manners.

> *Modern religion has ceased to be*
> *a religion at all. It has become*
> *a set of table manners.*

At the rambunctious heart of humanity, religion has always been about the supernatural commerce with the gods. Forget table manners. Furious, fiery beings were there to be wrestled with. A great war between heaven and earth was enjoined. The great dragon was engaged. Sacrifices were made. Blood was shed. Teenagers sang through torture. Old men smiled at their executioners and blessed the head of the one who would cut off their own heads. Holy men cracked jokes while they were grilled alive and scoffed at the terror of the scaffold. Housewives went into the flames with forgiveness on their lips or had their heads detached with a calm air of dignified detachment.

This willingness to wade into war is the poetical heart of religion. As Christ himself said, "I have not come to bring peace, but a sword."[3] So the religious romantic, like the poetic chevalier Cyrano de Bergerac, must not only wield a pen but a weapon. He must be a master not only of wordplay but of swordplay.

THE POINT OF
THE SWORD

THE MOUSE THAT ROARS

Fighting the Good Fight

C. S. Lewis, himself a romantic warrior, invented a classic hero in his valiant mouse Reepicheep. Reepicheep, who only comes up to a man's waist (Narnian talking mice are bigger than the terrestrial sort), brandishes his rapier to challenge every boorish act, rude word, or cowardly decision he encounters. In *The Voyage of the Dawn Treader*, Reepicheep is always the one to lead the charge, joust with giants, and engage the enemy in battle. At the end of the story, he paddles his small boat to the edge of the world and launches fearlessly into unknown realms.

Reepicheep is a mouse that roars—a whiskered chevalier as proud of his tail as Cyrano is of his nose. Lewis's making him a mouse was a stroke of genius as profound as Edmund Rostand's giving Cyrano his preposterous nose. That this noble musketeer is a mouse—the most timid of creatures—is an indication of what sort of person the romantic warrior needs to be if he or she is to not only fight the good fight but fight it well.

Before one can consider how to fight, it is necessary to remind ourselves that we must fight. Unfortunately, battle is not only necessary but unavoidable. The need for battle is based in that old but worthy saying, "All that it takes for evil to triumph is for enough good men to do nothing." Put simply, if we believe in good and evil, then we must admit that being a warrior is part of our duty. If we believe in good and evil, then it is obvious that evil will attack the good because that is what evil does. Therefore, we must be ready for the attack. If we believe in good and evil, then we must wish to be good. If we wish to be good, then we must confront evil because that is what good people do. And if we are going to confront evil, then we must be engaged in battle against evil.

> *If we believe in good and evil,*
> *then we must admit that being*
> *a warrior is part of our duty.*

Neat Nietzsche

Sadly, there are some who wish to deny the existence of good and evil. In a very neat argument, the philosopher Friedrich Nietzsche said that good and evil were simply illusions that developed from the facility of language. His argument goes like this: Language involves choice. A selection of sounds is designated as the name for a particular thing. Language is full of such choices. As soon as a choice is made, the notion of good and evil is implied, since to choose one thing over another implies that the thing you have chosen is better than the thing you have not chosen. Therefore, soon after language was created, we started to think of some things as "good" and other things as "evil." Nietzsche reasoned that good and evil were therefore simply illusions—by-products of our facility to use language.

The argument is fascinating, but it can be stood on its head quite simply. What if it were the other way around and the development of language came about because choice was possible, and choice was only possible because good and evil were already in existence? To put it more simply, it is just as likely that we developed the ability to use words and make choices because, from the very beginning, we were destined to choose between good and evil.

Nietzsche should have pondered the Genesis story a bit more. In that story the first parents were told not to eat of the tree of the knowledge of good and evil, indicating in that primitive and beautiful story that the nature of choice was locked into the reality of good and evil all along.

Others deny the reality of good and evil by saying that they are arbitrary value judgments that depend totally on one's point of view. What is good for me is good. What is bad for me is bad. This idea is too simple. It does not account for reality, for in every society, what we call the ultimate "good" is invariably not good for the individual. So, for example, all people believe cowardice is bad and courage is good, but courage requires self-sacrifice. It requires me to endanger my life, and if I go so far as to give up my life for others, then I am considered to be best of all. Furthermore, the idea of self-sacrifice rather than self-preservation runs through every dimension of our ideas of "goodness."

The Reality of Evil

These arguments are fascinating for philosophers, but in real life can anyone really deny the reality of good and evil? We may create complicated philosophical arguments that show good and evil to be merely constructs of the mind. We may say that what is good or evil simply depends on one's point of view, but all these clever arguments fade away when someone abducts, rapes, and murders a ten-year-old girl and throws her into a ditch. At that point we do not say that the rapist's actions were neutral but we simply perceive them to be evil because of a hiccup in our linguistic formation.

When we see an African woman with no hands trying to cuddle her baby—then learn that her hands were cut off by the very soldiers who gave her the baby by raping her—we do not stand back and philosophize about the difficulty of moral judgments. No, at that point we admit that there is such a thing as evil in the world, and if we are human, we do so with tears of a terrible and impotent rage.

We admit that there is such a thing as evil in the world, and if we are human, we do so with tears of a terrible and impotent rage.

At that point we recognize not only that there is such a thing as evil but that it is pervasive and aggressive—otherwise it would not be evil. We realize with sudden, stomach-lurching reality that the hideous cancer of evil has infiltrated every aspect of life on earth. It has wound its vile tentacles into every life, including yours and mine. Furthermore, this evil is aggressive. It is trying to dominate and destroy as much good as possible.

The romantic sees this evil, but he does not take the view that all is evil. He sees the evil, but he also sees the good. He sees the demonic actions of the African soldier, but he also sees, with tears in his eyes, the image of that woman with no hands still trying to caress her child. At that point the romantic rises up and vows to avenge such a terrible act and to put right such terrible wrongs.

The Wounded Warrior

There is a problem, however, with the righteous warrior. Those who believe they are serving a righteous cause often commit the greatest atrocities. The self-righteous warrior is the most frightening because he believes he can do no wrong. God is not on the side of any warrior who believes God is on his side. The truly romantic warrior sees the evil in the world and wants to fight it, but first of all he sees the evil in himself and wants to fight it. He realizes that he cannot hope to change the world if he cannot change himself.

The truly righteous warrior, therefore, is not a person who knows he is right but a person who knows he is wrong. The righteous warrior realizes he is a hypocrite. He knows that in a dark corner of his own life, he is just as capable of monstrous crimes as the worst of humanity. In other words, the righteous warrior may be full of confidence, but he is also full of humility. In fact, the true warrior's confidence is based in his humility. The truly humble person is not a groveling, subservient doormat. Instead he is fully aware of his strengths but also equally aware of his weaknesses. That is why he goes forward with both consummate confidence and consummate caution.

This is why Reepicheep is another great model of the romantic warrior. Is Reepicheep a man or a mouse? He is a mouse who is more courageous than the men he journeys with because he knows he is a mouse. The romantic warrior always remembers that he is a mouse, and that is why he brandishes his weapons with such panache, such bravery, and such foolish abandon. Put simply—he has nothing to lose. Because of his humility he can always admit that he was wrong—he knew that already. Because of his humility he can have a sense of humor; after all, *humility* and *humor* are both related to the word *humus*, which means "soil" or "earth." Because the warrior knows he is from the earth, he is always down-to-earth.

It is no mistake that all the great romantic heroes are warriors. Whether it is Indiana Jones or Jason, Odysseus or d'Artagnan, Luke Skywalker or the Lone Ranger, Cyrano or Zorro, the romantic heroes wear armor, ride out to battle, and wield the weapons of war. Without exception and without cowardice, they set out to do battle with dragons, criminals, monsters, and men. All the great stories communicate the one great story: that life is a battle between good and evil, and the part you play in that battle matters both here and hereafter.

> *All the great stories communicate the one great story: that life is a battle between good and evil, and the part you play in that battle matters both here and hereafter.*

However, with his strength every romantic hero carries a weakness; he nurses a wound and aches with some tragic flaw. The way he treats his weakness distinguishes him from the villain. The villain is never a total monster. He is a hero gone wrong. He is a romantic hero who has given in to the dark side of the force. The villain has ceased to fight against evil—most importantly, he has ceased to fight against the evil within himself. He is a villain because he has no self-doubt. He has forgotten that he has a flaw; indeed, what should be his aching wound has become the defining characteristic of the villain. At some point he stopped fighting the darkness within and so became one with the darkness without. Because the villain refused to dominate his dark side, it has dominated him.

If we wish to be good, the fight is before us. That does not mean that the fight is easy or secure. We are right to draw back from the call to be a romantic hero. We are right to doubt our worthiness for battle, but if we doubt our own integrity, it is a sign that we will be the right kind of warrior because we are less likely to be self-righteous. If we believe that we might do wrong, it is more likely that we will do what is right.

> *If we believe that we might do wrong, it is more likely that we will do what is right.*

If we get involved in the battle, we may worry that we will fight with mixed motives. We may worry that we have no skill or strength for battle. We may resort to the enemies' weapons, fighting with dishonesty, dirty tricks, and underhand tactics. We complain that the fight will be messy. Of course it will. It's a fight. There are blood, bashes, and broken teeth in a fight. We worry that we will get hurt. Of course we will get hurt. It's a fight. People get wounded. Some are killed.

When faced with the need to fight against evil, the greatest worry is that our cause is not just. This, too, is a fair concern. Usually the battle lines are unclear. The enemy often seems like a friend, while the ones we thought were friends turn out to be the enemy. At times the enemy is revealed in all his monstrous rage, but more often he remains in disguise. He uses subterfuge and spies and black propaganda. But this, too, is part of the battle. Part of the fight is good intelligence, a clear vision, and a knowledge of what is just and unjust. Working out the justice of a cause is part of the cause, and how Reepicheep and Cyrano decided who was the enemy and where the next battle lay was part of their genius as romantic heroes.

IDEALS, IDEOLOGIES, AND IDOLS

The Fight for Life

In *Fiddler on the Roof,* the jolly Jew Tevye sings a magnificent toast: "To life! To life! L'chaim!"[1] He sings his anthem to life at his daughter's wedding in the midst of grinding poverty, persecution, and pogroms. His praise of life and love and all things illimitably yes[2] is all the more poignant and powerful because he sings with joy from a broken heart. This is the song of the true romantic: a song with zest for life in the midst of heartache and disappointment.

Although Tevye longs to be a rich man, he does not sing

in praise of riches. He sings in praise of Life. It is true that he longs to be a rich man, but beneath that is his passion for life in whatever form it comes to him. Life is first. Life is basic. As a Jew, Tevye's hymn to life is especially poignant, because at the end of the play he is expelled from his home simply for being a Jew, and his expulsion from czarist Russia in the early 1900s is a harbinger of the later, more extreme expulsion of the Nazis' "final solution."

Tevye's toast to life is all the sharper because of the forces of death that are arrayed against him. For whatever particular reasons the czars or the Nazis persecuted the Jews, the underlying reason is that they regarded certain human beings as disposable. They understood their cause to be more important than life itself. That is to say, they had a cause that was more important than individual people's lives. They had a cause that kills, or if you like, they had a cause with claws.

A cause with claws invariably springs from a human longing from which a lofty ideology is born. No one sets out to commit mass murder; instead, tyrants commit genocide to follow through with their ideology, which was born of a lofty longing. History shows that mass murder can result from most any ideology. It could be a religious ideology. It could be a political ideology. It could be an economic ideology. It could be an ideology about class or caste. It could be an ideology about racial superiority, or it could be a combination of all these ideologies, but whatever and wherever and whenever the ideology, it is invariably an ideology that conceives a better life for all. But invariably the ideology that promises a better life for all is delivered by making sure there is no life for some.

*Invariably the ideology that promises
a better life for all is delivered by
making sure there is no life for some.*

For example, the Nazis wanted to make the world a better place. To reach their lofty longing, they developed an ideology to establish a superior race of human beings. Therefore, those who were inferior were to be eliminated. The Marxists and French Revolutionaries also wanted a better world. Their ideology was an economic and social system where all were equal, so they killed the economic overlords and those who were socially superior. The Ku Klux Klan desired a purer racial system, so those who were of the wrong color were eliminated. Communist atheists wanted a superior humanistic society, so those who believed in God were eliminated. At least these other ideologies had lofty aims—they wanted to create a better human race or a better world. The ideology of our own society is the most boorish and vulgar of all—we wish to enjoy total individual sexual freedom, so those who impede that (the unborn) are eliminated. Thus it is that every human ideology that strives sincerely for a better life ends up destroying life. Those ideologues who dream of a better humanity inevitably end up killing humans.

Ideals and Ideologies

The reader may protest, "But each of these ideologies sprang from such lofty longings! They promised so much! Their dreamers and poets and philosophers worked to make the world a better place. Their foot soldiers and devotees were passionate in the pursuit of their dreams. Were not these aspiring and inspiring dreamers the romantic warriors you are praising? Were they not willing to make the final sacrifice themselves to usher in their various versions of a brave new world? Are not the horrible examples you give proof against you? Are you not showing that these dreamers kill and commit the most horrific atrocities in the name of their ideals?" We must remember the difference between ideals and ideologies.

The ideologue's lofty longing is to make this world a better place. That is because he does not believe in a better world. In other words, he does not believe in a world other than this one, so all he can do is enforce an ideology to make this world better. The religious romantic, on the other hand, is not an ideologue but an idealist because he believes there is a better world than this one. He does not try to create a perfect world here because he believes there is a perfect, ideal world in the hereafter, and he aims to go there.

The religious romantic rejects ideologies because they are idols. In other words, they are false gods. Ideologues attempt to create heaven here on earth, and their ideologies, like all false gods, demand far more than they deliver, and what they demand is life itself. Just as certainly as the false gods of paganism demanded the bloody sacrifice of children, so the idolatrous ideologies demand blood. Push any ideology far enough and you will find violence, murder, mayhem, and genocide. This is because idealogues live for an idea—they do not live for life—and any ideology that does not put life first will invariably put it last. Similarly the good cause that does not first decide what is highest good will end up being bad.

Idealogues live for an idea—they do not live for life—and any ideology that does not put life first will invariably put it last.

The religious romantic rejects the idolatrous ideologies, not only because they are false gods, but because they are false goods. The ideologies are untrue, and because they are untrue, they are ultimately unreal. The romantic is an idealist because he believes in a world that is not only better but truer, and because it is truer, it is also more real. To make my point, we must abandon for a moment the picture of the romantic as a swaggering musketeer and cast him as a philosopher with a long, gray beard, a long black robe, and a longer speech.

"What is an ideal?" asks the romantic gray beard in the best tradition of the philosopher.

"An ideal is a striving for what is beautiful, good, and true," we reply.

"And what is beautiful, true, and good?" asks our romantic philosopher.

"That which is real is beautiful, true, and good," we reply.

"And what is real?"

"That which lasts forever is real."

"And what is it that lasts forever?" says the romantic philosopher with a quizzical glint in his eye.

"That which has no beginning or end."

"Is there such a Being that has no beginning and no end?"

At this point we throw up our hands and say, "Now you are discussing theology, not philosophy!"

Nevertheless, the question is necessary. The romantic follows an ideal because he believes in a world that is better than this one because it is a world that lasts forever. In other words, he believes there is such a thing as an eternal realm. The ideologue believes only in this world, and it is because he only believes in this world that he happily wreaks havoc among humanity.

What wringing of hands there is whenever there is genocide in the world! "How could ordinary people have allowed the horrors of Auschwitz?" we cry. "How could they kill so many innocent people in the gulag, the Killing Fields of Cambodia, Rwanda, or China? How could it happen?" The answer is this: everyone is motivated to action by his or her beliefs. To understand why anything happens, one has to consider the beliefs of the people who make it happen. When it comes to belief systems, at the base there are really only two to choose from: the physical or the metaphysical. You either believe that the physical world is the only real world, or you believe that in addition to the physical world, there is a metaphysical or invisible world that is even more real.

Better Worlds and Killing Fields

If you believe that the physical world is the only world, then you are correct to do everything you can to make the physical world a better place. Furthermore, since you are not going to be in this physical world for very long, you had better be quick about it. Time is not on your side. You are going to die within a few short years, so if this world is going to be improved, and your lot in this world is going to be improved, speed is essential.

If you believe that this world is the only world, then there is another very important negative belief that you also hold. You do not believe that you have a soul. There is no invisible part of you that goes on living after death. There is no heaven. There is no hell. There is no judgment. The result of this is that it does not really matter what you do here on this earth.

The result of not believing in your own soul is that you do not believe anyone else to have a soul either. Consequently, what does it matter if you kill another person? "Ah, what a brutal picture you paint!" I hear you protest, but the logic is inescapable. If there is no eternal soul, no hell to pay, no heaven to win, no consequence, why should not the strong take the life of the weak in order to create what seems to be a better world?

> *The result of not believing in your own soul is that you do not believe anyone else to have a soul either.*

There is no great mystery to genocide. There is no terrible riddle to cause us to wring our hands with dismay. It is all quite simple: those who commit genocide do not believe in the human soul and do not believe in eternal consequences, because all they believe in is the physical realm. If you only believe in the physical realm, why should you believe in the intrinsic worth of another human life? It's not going to last forever. If it is a nuisance or an obstruction to your plans, remove it as you would remove a troublesome tooth. Genocide for the secular materialist is no worse than pulling weeds.

Life Everlasting

The person, on the other hand, who believes in both the physical and the metaphysical believes that each human being is of eternal worth because at the heart of that being burns an eternal flame. Each human being has a soul, and each human being has a future. The believer in the metaphysical also believes that there is an unbreakable link between the physical and the metaphysical, between the visible realm and the invisible realm. What he does here matters hereafter. What he does in this life echoes into the next. If a man really believes in his own soul and the soul of his neighbor, then he will think twice before killing his neighbor.

Now it is easy to see why atheists find genocide an easier pastime than theists do. It is also easy to see how a belief in a metaphysical world has certain benefits. If you believe that you may pay eternally in the invisible realm for what you have done in the physical realm, it will function as a very nice deterrent to murder. However, one must not believe in the metaphysical realm simply because it is a useful deterrent to genocide. We must believe (or not believe) in the metaphysical realm not because it is useful but because it is true.

Is it true? I propose that there is a metaphysical realm not because of death but because of Life. Life itself demands that there is more to life than meets the eye. By *Life*, I am not referring to your life or to my life or to the life of a grasshopper or the life of a dahlia or the life of the owl at night, but to all of Life. The philosophers sensed that in and through and above and beyond each particular life was a force that was greater than them all, and on which all of them depended. Heraclitus suggested that the force was fire. The fire surged within all things but was greater than all things.

They believed in this "life force" because they saw that while all particular things died, Life still went on, and the Life that went on went on its own way. There was an unpredictability to this life force, almost as if it had a mind of its own. While the life force was greater than each particular life, it also lived within each particular life. If this was so, then each particular life shared, in some way, in the greater life force. If it shared in the greater life force, then it must also share in the transcendent and eternal dimension of that life force.

The idea that life goes on after death is not, as some shallow people think, simply a case of wishful thinking among superstitious, simple-minded, religious people. Life itself is a mysterious energy, and there is good reason to understand it as something that is bigger and better than the simple biological functions of any living being. If this is true, even in a very basic way, then we must start to imagine that there may be something after all about the metaphysical belief that is more than a practical deterrent to genocide.

Life itself is a mysterious energy, and there is good reason to understand it as something that is bigger and better than the simple biological functions of any living being.

If there is a life that is beyond our lives, then our noble and romantic quest is the quest to find that elusive mystery and give our whole physical lives in pursuit of that greater metaphysical life.

Just how we do this is the romance of religion.

8

BEATRICE, BEASTS, AND BEAUTY

The Fight for Beauty

When he was barely nine years old, the poet Dante glimpsed a beautiful young girl called Beatrice. He was intrigued. He was transfixed. He was transported, transposed, and transformed by her beauty. What might have been nothing more than a schoolboy's crush turned into a lifelong search, not just for a beautiful girl, but for beauty. Dante was one of the world's great romantic heroes. A warrior poet, he went through heaven and hell in search not only of beauty but of Love and Truth, and it was Beatrice who led him through it all.

The man from Missouri—that down-to-earth doubter,

that terrestrial Thomas—is not a bad man but a man who is naturally practical and not poetical. When considering Dante and his soulful search for beauty, the man from Missouri will object: "Hold on there! That Italian boy was jus' too dreamy for his own good. He only saw the girl once when he was nine, and he never even talked to her. Then once when he was eighteen she smiled and said, 'Good morning.' That's it. There was nothing more to it. He had a dumb schoolboy crush on the girl. He should've got over it." Yes, of course Dante was a fool for love, and that was exactly the correct response. Shall we kill love with logic or ridicule romance with ruthless reason? Those of us who love Dante know that he married another girl named Gemma, and they had some children and a decent marriage. Still, the figure of Beatrice drove the heart of his desire. There was something about the girl. What was it?

The boy was intrigued by the translucent. He was transfixed by the transcendent. It was not a beautiful girl he saw but eternal beauty in and through the girl. In daring to share his translucent and transcendent moment, he not only revealed that everlasting beauty is communicated through ordinary things, but he also revealed that an ordinary child of nine can perceive this truth. Dante redeems every geeky boy whose pimply jaw has dropped open at the beauty of a girl. He also redeems every child of every age who has ever, in whatever way imaginable, been transfixed even for a moment by beauty in all its forms. His irrational fixation was not on Beatrice but on beauty. This irrational fixation turned into desire, and his desire turned into determination, and this determination to follow his desire created his destiny to become the greatest poet and one of the greatest souls of all.

Beatrice and the Beautiful

Lest I get carried away with such a rhapsody on the theme of beauty, I should stop and acknowledge a few probing questions. Why did Dante consider Beatrice to be beautiful? Let us assume that Beatrice was classically beautiful, like her image in the pre-Raphaelite painting by Rossetti. She had flaming red hair, a long neck, a regal nose. She had heavy lids and open lips. She was breathtaking. Now, I regard such a female as beautiful, and so did Dante, and so may you, but was Beatrice really beautiful, or did Dante merely perceive her as beautiful? Is beauty a relative thing? Is beauty really only in the eye of the beholder?

> *Is beauty a relative thing? Is beauty really only in the eye of the beholder?*

It would seem so, for feminine beauty in other cultures is very different. An African tribal chieftain considers his girl beautiful if she has a bald head and a five-inch disc in her bottom lip. A Japanese man may be in ecstasy over a geisha girl, whose white face makes her look, to me, like a circus clown. A Burmese man wants his wife to have her neck stretched high with brass rings, while the Muslim man finds a woman he cannot see at all (because she is shrouded from head to toe in a burka) to be totally beautiful. Furthermore, within my own culture there are different tastes in female beauty. Some swoon at the sight of a skeletal waif. Others faint at the fuller female figure. If this is so, then beauty must be an individualistic matter of taste and conditioning by culture.

Or then again, not. We have gotten the wrong answer because we asked the wrong question. Instead of asking, "What is beautiful?" we should ask, "Why is anything beautiful at all?" It is true that the Muslim, the African, the American, and the Burmese all have very different standards for feminine beauty, but what they all agree on is that women are beautiful. What intrigues me is not the fact that one man fancies a woman with neck rings and another with earrings, or that one man finds a girl with a white face attractive while another likes a girl with a black face. What intrigues me is that men find women to be beautiful at all. Why should a man find a woman beautiful? What is this thing called *beauty*, and why do we feel such desire, such longing, and such yearning in the face of the beautiful?

> *What is this thing called* beauty,
> *and why do we feel such desire,*
> *such longing, and such yearning*
> *in the face of the beautiful?*

The psychological, anthropological, historical, practical, analytical man will stroke his goatee and say, "Ahh, now . . . Why does the male of the species find the female of the species beautiful? It is because he finds her attractive. And why does he find her attractive? I'm afraid there is nothing mysterious about it. The answer is hormones. Nothing more. The male is attracted to the female because he wants to mate with her. He is attracted to large breasts and wide hips because they exhibit her childbearing capacity. He likes red lips and wide eyes because they are the first signs of sexual arousal. Those other details? The neck bangles, the lip discs, and the diamond rings are all indicators of the girl's wealth. The Muslim's desire for his wife to wear a burka is a sign of her modesty and, therefore, her goodness and virtue. You see, this mysterious thing you call *beauty* can all be explained through anthropological, psychological, historical, and cultural observation."

Yes, yes . . . but the man doesn't say to himself, "There's a woman who will bear many strong sons!" Or "My, she's a wealthy lass; look at all those neck bangles." Or "I'm sure she'll be a modest and good woman, for she wears a burka." He simply gasps and says, "She's beautiful!" To be sure, the allure of the beautiful has everything to do with desire, and the most basic desire is sexual desire, and therefore what we think is beautiful is linked with what we find to be erotic.

The Erotic, the Erratic, and the Iconic

Unfortunately, what is erotic is also erratic. Beauty is inconsistent. It is unpredictable. It is impossible to pin down. Not only do men from different cultures and different ages find different traits in women beautiful, but beauty cannot be explained away by the erotic urge, for men find many things beautiful that they have no desire to mate with.

We may understand why Dante found Beatrice beautiful and write it off as nothing more than adolescent eroticism, but why does a man consider a rosebud to be beautiful? Why does he sigh at a sunset, languish at a landscape, marvel at a mathematical theorem, or go quiet in a cathedral? What is it in a sonnet or a symphony, a medieval Madonna, a Monet, or a Ming vase that can strike a man dumb with awe?

There is clearly something more to aestheticism than eroticism. What is it that makes a man bow down to beauty? The Eastern Orthodox monk may shed light on the matter. In his religion, he venerates icons. He kisses them and lights candles before them and fills his churches with them. Furthermore, he has a complex custom of how to paint the icons. Each stage—from making the brushes to mixing the paint—has its own prayer. Each stage of painting follows a carefully learned law and delicate discipline.

> *There is clearly something more*
> *to aestheticism than eroticism.*

In this archaic and arcane tradition, the Eastern Orthodox monk exhibits the true depth and meaning of all things that are beautiful. For the Eastern Orthodox, the icon is not only beautiful in itself; it is a window into something more beautiful. The iconic image of Blessed Mary Ever-Virgin is not just a pretty picture of a pretty girl. It is an image of blessedness, everlastingness, and cosmic purity. It is more than that: it is a channel through which the monk connects with blessedness and eternal purity. It is more than that: for the monk, it is a powerful token through which blessedness and eternal purity can be channeled into the world.

The icon is, therefore, not simply an image, but an image of all images, and therefore of all things beautiful. The icon, as a window to eternal beauty, teaches us that each thing we perceive as beautiful connects us with that which is eternally beautiful. We progress from the basics of beauty, which are mere eroticism, to the love of a beautiful figure, to the love of a beautiful object, to the love of all things beautiful, to the love of a person's inner beauty, which leads to the love of virtue and finally to the love of the source of virtue and the source of beauty itself. This pilgrim's progress is proof, far greater than a rational proof, for the existence of the eternal. It is proof not from the mind of man but from the heart of humanity. The existence of beauty is a proof for existence of the transcendent, because it is an experience universal in time and space, and universal to the whole human race. It is as undeniable and unexplainable as love, for that, too, is common to all men and so transcends each man. This is why the quest for beauty lies at the heart of the romance of religion.

Beauty and the Beast

This is why the romantic hero always seeks to save the fair maiden. Do not imagine that he is simply on a quest to find a good wench and have a tumble in the hay. His quest is far more noble than that. The romantic hero is an unworthy suitor. He is humbled by his beloved and humbles himself in her presence. He is the beast searching for beauty, and his poignant search for beauty is also a quest to be saved by beauty. This is why he writes sonnets and why his heart is broken by the torture of love. It is because the sight of beauty reveals what a beast he really is and calls him to go on a quest, not only to find beauty, but once found, to embrace beauty. In that embrace he will be so consumed by beauty that he is transformed, as if by magic, and ceases to be beastly and becomes beautiful himself.

This romantic quest lies at the heart of every great story because it lies at the heart of humanity itself. In the face of this heart-wrenching saga, we must ask what the atheistical, analytical, practical, cynical man has to offer. What explanation has he for the mystery of beauty? What theory can he offer for the surge in the human heart in the face of beauty? Where does this come from? What evolutionary hiccup caused such a phenomenon? What is the psychological, anthropological, analytical answer to this conundrum? I can think of none.

The Mystery of Mysticism

Once again, the problem is not that the critics and cynics are critical and cynical but that they are not critical and cynical enough. They have not been critical of their own criticism, nor cynical about their cynicism. The problem is not that they have asked questions but that they have not asked enough questions. It is said that the cynic sees through everything, but this is exactly what the cynic does not do. He does not see through a thing enough. That is to say, he has not seen through a thing to see what is beyond. The cynic is like a man who looks into a window and sees only glass.

The cynic is like a man who looks into a window and sees only glass.

Instead, the mystics and the poets and the children were right. They understood that to really see something was to see something more. It is quite simple: when we behold the beautiful, we gaze on something greater than we are. We connect with the infinite. We transcend this physical world and look through a window into a world beyond. Even the doubtful philosopher Schopenhauer believed that the experience of the beautiful helped one transcend the selfish will and enter into a moment he called "pure perception."[1] Pure perception might be called "a greater way of seeing" or a way not of seeing through something but seeing into it.

I said that the physical man must learn to see what is invisible. This is how it is done—when we perceive beauty, we do just that: we see what is invisible coming to us through that which is visible. This process is otherwise called *mysticism*. Mysticism is not mystical at all, and it is certainly not very mysterious. It is the ordinary, practical experience that every man enjoys when he knows that lift of the heart, that inexplicable sense of joy, that transcendent moment when, through the apprehension of beauty, he connects with the infinite; when through the glimpse of visible beauty he glimpses what is beautifully invisible.

This life-changing experience is what the romantic hero knows is true. It validates his quest and confirms his deepest suspicions. Beauty opens the way for him to meet the one great thing he is searching for: the mystery that is beautiful beyond beauty: the even greater mystery of Love.

HOLLYWOOD HEROES AND HARLEQUIN ROMANCE

The Fight for Love

My friend Carol is a writer of medical romantic fiction. This does not mean that she writes warmhearted prose about anatomical procedures; she does not pen sugary sagas about surgery or candlelight accounts of cardiac attacks. No, she writes "female fiction," known in the trade as Harlequin romance. She writes about nurses who are in love with doctors, physiotherapists who fall for family physicians, and pretty technicians with crushes on chiropodists. Carol produces salable, sentimental entertainment for females. She writes unashamedly about the search for love, and her books sell.

It is easy for the tasteful to turn up their fine-tuned noses at Carol's craft. They scorn her common turn of phrase. They disdain the Harlequin romance. They sneer at Carol's heart-throbbing heroines with their happy endings. The literati smile condescendingly at her gift to write for hoi polloi, and chuckle at the simple sentimentality of her stories: "These are comfort books for sad, fat, abandoned women who consume them as fast as they do a box of chocolates. The women and the books and the chocolates are all alike: they are gooey, sweet, and have soft centers." The aesthetes and literati may keep their tasteful snobbery to themselves. I am on the side of Carol and all her readers, for together they keep alive in this cruel and cynical world the glorious tackiness of romance.

The literati are similarly snobbish about another genre of popular romance—the heroic Hollywood movie. The critics sneer at superheroes and simplistic plots. They deride the fact that the knight always slays the dragon to rescue the damsel in distress. The cowboy always rides off into the sunset with his woman, the hard-hearted hero always finds love, the good guy always gets the girl, and the good woman always stands by her man. Popular movies are simply heroic, romantic tales for men. They are for the guys what Carol's books are for the girls: romance for the rabble.

I raise my glass to the rabble. I salute the common man and woman who love sentimental stories and romantic tales, because they are the majority. As a rule, I am suspicious of majority rule. I doubt whether the majority are right about many things, but I don't doubt that they are right when it comes to matters of the heart. The fact that ordinary women buy millions of copies of medical romances, and ordinary men flock to movies where the hero always kills the bad guy and embraces the beautiful woman, reminds me that the search for love is a universal component of humanity.

> *The search for love is a universal component of humanity.*

The Caramel-Centered Hero

The soft-centered lovers of popular romance remind me of Cyrano de Bergerac's soft-centered friend Ragueneau—the poetical pastry chef. An extravagant connoisseur of both poetry and pastry, the fat chef loves sweets for the stomach and sweets for the heart and mind. He combines sonnets with sugar icing and terza rima with a raisin twist. This poet with a *pain au chocolat* is Cyrano's sidekick, a French Sancho Panza—a Samwise Gamgee of the patisserie.

The hero's sentimental sidekick often plays the part of a wise fool. He is himself a jester, a harlequin, and a clown because he holds out for his ideals. He fights for the right in the face of defeat. He does not bow to the wise and mighty but stands at the side of his hero, knowing that to do so is foolishness but that the wisdom of the world is always confounded by the foolishness of God.

I am the defender of the readers of romantic novels, the moviegoing male, and the soft-centered sidekicks who are usually pleasantly plump. I defend the pudgy Sancho Panzas, the rotund Ragueneaus, and the sentimental Samwise Gamgees of the world. They are a commonplace of romantic literature; and if they are a commonplace, then they are common; and if they are common, then I salute them because they stand for the common man. If they love sentimental tales, romantic fiction, and movies with tearjerker endings, that is only because they have large and tender hearts. They believe in something called love, and they know that the search for love is the one great romantic quest of them all. And if they do not succeed in that quest, they have not succeeded in life.

I am for the ordinary, soft-centered sidekick because he stands for that passionate and pudgy soul who stands at the side of every romantic hero. Indeed, he stands at the hero's side as a kind of alter ego. He stands at the hero's side because he is the other side of the hero. In fact, he is not only the other side of the hero—he is the inside of the hero. That is to say, he stands for the soft center at the heart of the hero himself, for underneath the swagger and the swordplay, the romantic hero swoons. Beneath the bluster is a blossoming flower. Underneath the tough exterior is a tender heart.

Hearts and Hot Pants

This is the puzzle at the heart of the romantic quest: that the romantic quest has a heart. This is a mystery that very few people have stopped to examine: all of us assume the existence of this thing called "love" and that it is a great good, a prize to be won, a gift to be given, a reward to be earned. We take it for granted that our stories will be about brave men who endure great ordeals to win the hands of their ladies. We accept, without question, the romantic tales of windblown women on rocky cliffs and dark heaths who will be swept up into the arms of men named Darcy, Rocky, and Heathcliffe. But why should there be such a thing as "love" at all? Why should humanity be gripped with such a yearning to belong and such a longing for love?

> *Why should there be such a thing as "love" at all? Why should humanity be gripped with such a yearning to belong and such a longing for love?*

The atheist or anthropologist will no doubt find a simple biological answer: the infant remembers the warm embrace of the mother's womb and seeks for a similarly secure embrace. The child remembers the warm sweetness of suckling the breast and seeks a similar sweetness in adulthood. "Love," argue the psychologist and sociologist, "is no more than the desire to be loved, and the desire to be loved is no more than the innocent desire to be sheltered from the dark and stormy night, to be nurtured and looked after. Love is simply the thrill that someone will give me supper." It would seem to be true: what I thought was true love turns out to be cupboard love.

Then there is the erotic explanation for love: it is not only the desire for someone to give me supper and tuck me up tight in bed; it is also the desire to be tucked up tightly with someone else in bed. The desire to be embraced and to embrace is really the desire to embrace another in the sexual act. According to this theory, my love for the girl in hot pants is really no more than my own hot panting. In other words, love equals sex. No more. No less.

Both of these explanations are variations on a theme. They both explain this desire we call "love" as projected personal requirement. I don't love another person; I love the pleasure that other person represents. I do not love the person; I love what that person can offer me. I do not love that other person; I love sex and my supper. While this is a conclusion with which many a jaded wife might agree, we must not let them get away with it, for love is something more.

While many emotions perceived as "love" can be explained with these crude theories, a problem remains, and the problem is this: everyone everywhere who believes in love believes that whatever love is, and wherever it comes from, what it most expressly is *not* is naked self-interest. All the great poets and preachers, all who have sighed and swooned and died and crooned about love, believe that love is not self-interested, but self-sacrificial. The most sublime lines on love have not been written about what the lover can get but about what the lover can give, and the greatest line on love of all is, "Greater love has no man than this, that a man lay down his life for his friends."[1]

Everyone everywhere who believes in love believes that whatever love is, and wherever it comes from, what it most expressly is not *is naked self-interest.*

Without doubt, this self-sacrificial love is debased into self-interest, but this is not love. It is lust. We have simply misunderstood a distinction in terms. If there is such a thing as love, then it is defined as being interested more in the welfare of the beloved than oneself, and if such a virtue exists, then the mystery of love becomes even greater.

Suddenly this great ideal lies at the heart not only of Carol's medical romances and the superhero movies but of humanity itself. The mystery deepens, for when we truly long for love, we do not long just for someone else to give themselves totally in love for us; we also long to give ourselves totally and completely to another. We want to be lost in love. We want to be submerged in love. We want to be overwhelmed by our own self-sacrifice and self-giving to the beloved. We want to die for love.

The Riddle of Sacrifice

Here is the puzzle: if the cynical unbeliever is right, how can a quality that is (by its definition) self-sacrificial have become the most sublime and foundational desire for a race of beings who, the evolutionist tells us, have survived by being the most viciously self-interested brutes in the jungle? In other words, how did the drive to survive by devouring others evolve into the overwhelming desire to give ourselves in sacrifice for others?

The anthropologist would offer a complicated attempt at an answer along the lines of, "Well, you see, individual early humanoids began to establish themselves in packs or tribes, and it soon became evident that it was better for the individuals if the whole tribe survived, so the self-interest of each individual became subordinated to the overall survival of the tribe, and roles began to be differentiated and prioritized so that an ideal of self-sacrifice for the good of the whole tribe became the most highly prized trait." Balderdash. Why, then, did chieftains still battle with chieftains for preeminence, and why did they despise the weak and the frail and kill them whenever they could?

No, the need to sacrifice oneself in love for another is so radical and revolutionary that it must be reality. In other words, the desire to sacrifice oneself for love is so otherworldly that it must have come from another world. It is so alien to the tooth and claw of natural selection that it must be the result of a supernatural selection.

> *The desire to sacrifice oneself for love is so otherworldly that it must have come from another world.*

Humanity is mystified by love. All humans experience it. None can explain it. The mysterious genesis of this strange gift, the wondrous beginnings of this bizarre quality within the human heart, prompts the greatest quest of all: the quest for love. This is a quest not only to find true love but to find where such love comes from and to understand such a great and bewildering mystery. Why, when all my animal instincts drive me to self-preservation, should I reach out to rescue another? Why, when every childlike desire for pleasure and safety controls me, should I long to give myself to another? Why, when the jungle beast within snarls at every threat, do I wish to calm the monster and seek to sacrifice myself for love?

This mystery is at the heart of the romantic quest, and this is why in all the great romances there is romance. At the heart of all the great stories there is a love story. The greatest heroes have hearts that are smitten. They do what they do for the love of their lady, but not just for the love of the lady, but for the love of love.

The hero dies for love because he knows that this quest leads him from earthly love to heavenly love.

The Sacred Heart

To get a glimpse of what this means, we need to stop for a moment and ask what it is that drives all things and keeps all things alive. This force may be called Energy. Heraclitus called it Fire. The Hebrews called it Wisdom. The Greek philosophers called it Logos. Christians call it Love. Divine love is the energy by which all things were created and by which all things consist. Divine love, as Dante sings, is "the Love that moves the sun and the other stars."[2] Could it be that at the heart of Carol's medical romances where the girl gets the guy, at the heart of the Hollywood movies where the guy gets the girl, there is a sacred heart—a heart that stirs the force that moves the sun and the other stars?

If such a precious idea is true, or even if one believes it to be true, then we can see why all the worlds' heroes bear a sword. This most precious gift of love is the greatest treasure and is worth the most dangerous quest. If earthly love connects us with eternal love, then it connects us with eternal life; and that most precious gift is something that is not only worth a long journey; it is also worth a fight. It is worth a fight because anything so precious must be surrounded by many thieves. Anything so good must be surrounded by much evil, for evil (by definition) wants to destroy what is good.

Therefore the romantic hero bears a sword as he sallies out to fight for love. As he does, he realizes that his battle for love and for beauty is pointless if all he is responding to are his vague emotions. He realizes that he cannot act on his heart alone. He must engage in an intellectual as well as a sentimental battle. He must know where he is going. He must have a map for his journey. His fluttering heart needs a philosophy. There must be method to his madness; there must be a reason for his romance. His quest has raised a question, and the question is as old as Pontius Pilate: "What is truth?"

TRUTH, TREASURE, MAPS, AND TRAPS

The Fight for Truth

When I was a boy, I had a Walt Disney long-playing record of the story of *Treasure Island*. The story had all the makings of a great heroic tale: truth, treasure, maps, and traps. Jim Hawkins is left a treasure map by a crusty old pirate. He sets off from his comfortable world on an adventure to overcome the pirates and not only to follow the map to find the treasure but also to find the truth about Treasure Island. The story, like all great heroic stories, is not just about the quest for hidden treasure but the quest for hidden truth. There is a mystery behind the treasure, and it is in solving the mystery and discovering the truth that the true treasure is found. Furthermore, it is the quest for the treasure and the truth that makes a man out of Hawkins the boy and helps him not only discover the treasure and the truth but also become a hero in the process.

This same quest for the treasure of truth is the romance of religion. There is much that can be said about the search for the treasure of truth, but it should first be established that there is really such a thing as truth. There are many who doubt if there is such a thing as objective truth. Instead, they think truth is a relative and rubbery thing. "What is true is what seems true to you, but your truth is not necessarily the same as my truth." This is absurd, and to state such a proposition is to disprove it, for how can something be "true for me and not for you"? If it is true, it is true for both of us. The relativist cuts off the branch he sits on, for he operates under the assumption that his own statement, "What is true for me is not true for you" is itself true. Therefore, if his relativistic statement is true, then there is such a thing as truth, and he is wrong. If he is really correct that "what is true for me is not true for you," then I may disagree that his statement is true and I will be as right as he is.

Because all the greatest religions are dogmatic, it is assumed that the religious man not only believes that there is such a thing as truth but has it all written down neatly in a book, and that all you need to do is read that book to know and understand all truth. This may be the case for some religious people, but they are not engaged in the romance of religion. They are engaged in the reduction of religion. They reduce the great romance of religion to a list of correct doctrinal statements and moral precepts. The rules may be right, but religion is more than the rules. Such people may be religious, but they are not romantics. They are the Puritans and Pharisees, the purse-lipped old grouches of religion.

However, when the religious romantic says that there is such a thing as truth, he is not necessarily saying that the truth is easy to discover, define, and defend. He wrestles with the difficulty that there are many different religions and that all of them have truth within them. He sees that the truth has many faces and wears many different costumes. He admits with the relativist that truth is difficult to find and know. This is precisely why he is a religious romantic—because he is on the quest to find the hidden treasure he calls truth. He knows that he does not know it all. He is agnostic about many things and curious about many more. He lives in an open-ended and wondering state of mind. Like Jim Hawkins, he has set out on a voyage to Treasure Island. The sea on which he sails is uncertain, and the ship in which he sails is uncertain, and as a sailor he is also uncertain. That is to say, he is uncertain about himself.

The Dogmatist and the Dogmatic Doubter

This is how the adventurer for truth differs from both the religious dogmatist and the relativist, for both the religious dogmatist and the relativist are not uncertain about them-selves. They may not know much, but they know one thing with absolute certainty: they know they are right.

However, unlike the relativist, there is one thing the religious romantic does believe, and this one belief is at the foundation of all the rest: he may be uncertain about himself, but he is certain that no matter how hard it is to discover, there really is a hidden treasure. There really is such a thing as truth, and it really can be discovered if one will only set out on the great adventure to find it.

This is where the religious hypocrite and the relativist are, like two madmen, standing back to back. Both of them are dogmatists. One knows he is a dogmatist; the other denies it. The religious hypocrite who trusts in his dogma knows that he is a dogmatist. In that respect, he is less dangerous than the relativist, who also thinks he knows everything but denies that he is a know-it-all. The man who thinks he knows everything may one day discover that he does not, but the man who is 100 percent convinced that there is no truth will never be able to acknowledge his error. In this respect, the relativist is far more of a fool than the religious dogmatist. He is absolutely dogmatic on his one unshakable "truth"—that there is no such thing as truth—and like all dogmatists, he has no shred of doubt about his foundational assumption. His colossal self-deception is compounded by the fact that this dogmatist does not regard himself as a dogmatist. Instead, he believes himself to be the father of all doubters. He has doubted all dogma except the one dogma he should have doubted: his dogma that there is no such thing as truth.

The Quest and the Questions

The religious romantic, on the other hand, is the one who truly questions. He questions as the curious child questions—because he wishes to understand. He questions because he is on a quest. He questions because he is curious. The religious romantic sets out on the great quest with two convictions: that there is such a hidden treasure as truth, and that he has been given a map to find it. The religious romantic does not consider his religion the end of the journey but the map for the journey. This is where the religious dogmatist differs from the religious romantic. The religious dogmatist believes he has already discovered the hidden treasure: it is his religion. Because he believes he has already discovered the treasure, he does not consider the journey necessary.

The religious romantic sets out on the great quest with two convictions: that there is such a hidden treasure as truth, and that he has been given a map to find it.

Modern people often blame religion for being dogmatic. That is because they (like many religious people) have not understood the true reason for dogma. The dogma and the moral precepts of religion are simply the map for the quest. The better the religion, the more precise and detailed the dogma, just as the better the map, the more precise and detailed it is. A religious romantic loves his dogma in a different way than the dogmatic religionist. He loves it as a cartographer loves a map—for the map's sake. He loves it because it unlocks a whole new world for him. The map, for the religious romantic, is a curious and colorful document that points the way and illustrates the journey. It has been composed for him by many ancient sages who have completed the journey before him. To study the map excites him because it points the way. It inspires his journey, it illuminates the quest, it guides the path, it opens the way before him. He loves to study the map. He venerates the map. He would never be without the map; he loves it not for itself but for where it leads him.

While the map may be true, the truth itself is not the map. Neither is the truth the religious dogma. The religious dogma is simply an expression of the truth. It is true—indispensably true—but truth is truer and bigger than dogma in the same way that a map is true, but the journey is truer and bigger than the map. The journey is a real experience. It is an encounter. It is an adventure. It is an experience so much greater and richer and deeper than any dogma can ever express or any map can ever recount.

> *While the map may be true, the truth itself is not the map.*

Truth as Person

When Pontius Pilate asked Jesus Christ, "What is truth?"[1] he was met with silence by the person who had already said, "I am the Truth." And the one who said, "I am the Truth" also said, "I am the Way."[2] In other words, truth is a process. Truth is a path. This is something the religious romantic understands at the heart of it all. He understands that truth can only be really known through the adventure. He must embark on the great quest with all his body, mind, and spirit, knowing that the truth is buried deep at the end of the journey. When he does find the treasure, he finds that X really has marked the spot. For X has always been the sign, not only of the hidden treasure, but of the treasure that is a cross; and on the cross is X, which is the secret symbol for *christos*, which is the name for the Christ.

This is why the religious romantic is engaged in a quest for the truth and also for beauty and love, because he knows that beauty, love, and truth cannot be divided. To find true beauty is to love it, and to find true love is to find truth, and to find truth is something beautiful and lovely. The three go together like a little holy Trinity. The religious romantic, therefore, embarks on his quest to discover truth in a series of philosophical or theological propositions. He does not believe that truth is simply a statement of beliefs or a diktat of discipline—a moral code to be obeyed. It is not less than these things but more than these things. Truth, he comes to discover, is an experience and an encounter with a person who is beauty, love, and truth together, and who calls himself "the Way."

Truth is found not just in a series of religious statements but within the full-blooded adventure of life itself.

This man who is Truth and Way also calls himself "the Life." In other words, the Truth is found not just in a series of religious statements but within the full-blooded adventure of life itself. The religious romantic experiences this full-blooded truth as a quest, as a life of encounter and a life of conflict, for to find the treasure of truth he must battle with pirates. He must go on a long voyage, wade through deep swamps, and cross the seas where the maps all say, "Here there be dragons."

This adventure is not for the fainthearted. It is not for those who know it all. It is not for those who seek a comfort zone. It is not for those who wish to take their ease in either a religious dogma or a relativistic dogma. It is a quest for the Reepicheeps, the Cyranos, the chevaliers and knights of the spirit. The religious romantic believes such a quest is possible, and the way he goes on this quest is through the practice of his religion. This is the way he sets off with a band of pirates and traitors to sail the high seas in search of the treasure of truth, and like every true adventurer, the religious romantic realizes that the journey is full of danger, dark and deep. If he would find the buried treasure, he must be prepared to dig, and that digging will take him down into the underworld—into the dark caverns of the mind where the deep, cold lakes are home to unimaginable monsters, and where the grim horrors of truth must be confronted.

THE POINT OF THE STORY

HOBBIT HOLES AND THE HOLY

The Way Down Is the Way Up

Once upon a time, a professor of philology—that is to say, a lover of language—was daydreaming in his university room when he scribbled on the back of an anonymous exam paper, "In a hole in the ground there lived a hobbit."[1] Thus was begun a true story—one of the greatest of the true stories ever told. A true story is a story that is true even if it is not factual. It doesn't just express truth or explain truth or argue for truth. It is simply true. It is true in a way that defies explanation and analysis and explication and argumentation. It is true because in its very fiber there is truth. It is true in its texture and structure. It is true through and through.

This kind of story is very rare in modern literature because the modern author either doesn't believe in truth at all or he believes in a watered-down sort of truth, which is usually no more than an ideology or a collection of catchphrases that feel like wisdom. While this sort of story is rare in the modern world, it was very common in the ancient world. The stories they told long ago were full of mystery, monsters, and magic. They were full of depth and darkness and delight. They were superabundant with the supernatural and overflowing with all that was awesome. The ancient tales were all about the interwoven mystery of gods and men. In them the mysterious realm was locked in an eternal interplay with the everyday world. In the old stories the invisible was alive within the visible, and human beings were players on a supernatural stage. In those stories the ideal throbbed within the real, and the dramatic interplay was constantly alive and frightening and unpredictable and exciting.

The true stories were constant pointers to the real possibility that the unseen world could intersect this world and that powerful forces were constantly at play influencing what seemed to be ordinary history. There was always something going on behind the scenes. There was always another level of meaning, a hidden truth, and a veiled presence.

The true stories were constant pointers to the real possibility that the unseen world could intersect this world and that powerful forces were constantly at play influencing what seemed to be ordinary history.

Where the Wild Things Are

This is why the hobbit (and Alice's rabbit) lived down a hole. The hole was the entrance to the underworld. This is why Dante went through a dark wood and found a hole down into the underworld. This is why Neo goes into the alternative world in *The Matrix*, and why Batman lives in a cave. The heroes were all going into that deep and dark world where the wild things are. They were going into the unknown. This quest down into the unknown world is a sign (in one way or another) of the task of the mythical hero. He must be a person of two worlds: the upper world that is seen and physical and the lower world that is unseen and spiritual. He must go from the conscious, with all its clarity, to the subconscious, with all its obscurity. In that sense the mythical hero is also a mystical hero, because he must go on an adventure into the mystical realm. He must be both a physical and a spiritual being.

When the hero goes down into the underworld, he is showing everyone who would be a religiously romantic hero that he, too, must go down into the depths. As Jesus Christ commanded his fishermen friends, "Cast out into the deep."[2] The ancient Hebrews were not seagoing people. They feared and dreaded the sea. For them it was the realm of the deepest and darkest things. There was the mighty Leviathan, the monster of the deep. Their prophet Jonah was cast into those depths and was swallowed up by the sea monster, only to rise again on the third day, covered with vomit but triumphant. This is the process of the romantic hero. He must go down to go up. He must face the dark to find the light. He must go into the underworld, like Orpheus, to rescue his beloved, and the beloved he rescues is life itself.

To translate all of this into more ordinary terms, it means that if we are going to embark on the journey, then we must be willing to face the dark, and the first dark we must face is the darkness within ourselves. This is not a task for cowards, and most of us are cowards. Furthermore, we know we are cowards and we know that we must face the dark. "Dark dark dark. They all go into the dark," spake the prophet Eliot.[3] So, instead of facing the path through the quagmire, where there is no foothold, we stay in the world of light, where we imagine we are safe, and we devise new and devious ways to deal with the dark: we project it onto others.

Instead of facing the darkness within ourselves, we see the darkness everywhere else but in ourselves. Of all the evils within the human heart, this is the deepest and the darkest evil, for when we project our own fears and unknown darkness onto others, then two dreadful things happen at once: we make others evil and ourselves good. As soon as we shift the darkness onto someone else, that person becomes the villain and we are launched upward into the exhilarating heights of fake self-glory and artificial goodness. This flight from the depths is the hallmark of the coward and the sign of the truly dreadful villain. This is why, in the great stories, the greatest villains think they are good, while the greatest heroes know they are not.

The great hero knows he is not good, because he has gone down into the dark underworld and found himself there. He has gone where the wild things are, and he has discovered that the wild thing is himself. The villain, on the other hand, is a big sissy. He is afraid of the dark—especially the darkness within himself. However, he pretends to be a big tough guy. He struts like Darth Vader, who justifies his evil and continues to pretend that he is good. He blames others. He fears others. He views everyone else as the enemy, and before long everyone else is his enemy.

Down Is Up

The hero, on the other hand, knows that he must go down into the depth, and he does so with the courage, beauty, and grace of the pearl diver. He sheds everything that holds him back, and he plunges naked and alone into the cold, dark depths. What does he find there? He finds the pearl of great price. He finds himself, but he also finds humility. Humility is a beautiful virtue, but it is also a beautiful word, for remember it means "earth" and is linked with the words *humus* and *humor.* The hero goes down into the underworld. In other words, he goes down into the earth—into the humus—and as he does he discovers humility and good humor. He crawls under the bed, where he thought there were monsters, and comes out the other side laughing, for all he finds is dust.

The startling truth about the religious hero, therefore, is that he is a man of the earth. Unlike the classical heroes, who hold their heads high with pride, the Christian hero holds his head high with laughter—laughter at the world, laughter at the pride of men, and laughter at himself. He has come to know himself, and what he knows is that he is a joke. He is laughable in his puny power and his high hopes, and because he laughs at himself, the Christian hero is above all heroes, the most dignified. It is only a humble person who can laugh at himself, and it is only the person who can laugh at himself who has the most dignity, for true dignity is based on true worth, and true worth is understood only in humility.

This is the essential story that has been told in every age and in every culture: the hero goes on a long journey to a distant, alien land. While the journey is outward and visible, the real journey is always inner and invisible. This is why the land where the hero goes is peopled with monsters, magic, wizards, and all kinds of wonders. In myths and tales of science fiction and fantasy, he goes to a strange and mysterious land because that represents the strange and mysterious land of the spirit that anyone who is truly human knows he must one day traverse.

Deep down within each one of us, we know that we must go into that strange and terrifying land. It is the adventure we were made for. It is our destiny and our darkest desire. We know that we must go into that dark and mysterious place because each one of us is haunted by the realization that sooner or later we will go into the Dark whether we want to or not; this time I mean Dark with a capital *D*, and the *D* stands not only for "dark" but for "death."

> *Deep down within each one of us, we know that we must go into that strange and terrifying land. It is the adventure we were made for. It is our destiny and our darkest desire.*

The trek into the unknown land, the way down into the dark, is the journey that awaits each one of us. The romantic hero always sets out on this journey alone, because each one of us knows that there is one journey we go on with no companions: the journey into the land of death. This looming presence, this ominous call, this persistent summons lurks like a shadow on the other side of every solid object and every ray of light in our lives.

The Dark and the Destiny

There are only two ways to deal with this reality and only one way to deal with it realistically. The first way to deal with this reality is to ignore it. This is what most people do most of the time. We really do imagine that Mr. Death will not stop at our house. We live our lives imagining and worrying about many things that will never happen, all the time ignoring the one thing that will most certainly happen.

The only realistic way to deal with the reality of death is to face it daily. The wiser men in ages gone by would keep skulls on their desks or skeletons in their closets. They were their memento mori—their daily reminders of death. Those who face death squarely have two ways to deal with it; one is wise and the other is foolish. The foolish man faces death but tells himself that after death there is nothing and that he will simply cease to exist. He accuses the man who believes in heaven of wishful thinking, but it seems to me that the man who believes that after his death he will simply cease to exist is the one who is thinking wishfully.

The vast majority of the human race alive now and in all ages and in all places have believed in some sort of afterlife.

From vampire legends to the tombs of the pharaohs, from belief in reincarnation and resurrection and tales of near-death experiences to visions of heaven and hell and stories of ghosts and ghouls—in a multitude of ways and expressions, the human race has been aware of some sort of existence after this existence is over. The man who wishes to simply cease to exist is wishing against all the evidence and experience of the whole human race.

> *The man who wishes to simply cease to exist is wishing against all the evidence and experience of the whole human race.*

The wise man weighs the evidence and experience and places Pascal's wager. Pascal was the one who said that, given the choice, the man who believes in the afterlife and a final judgment and lives accordingly will be the winner. If he is wrong, and there is nothing after death, then he has had a good life and lost nothing. On the other hand, if the man who believes there is no afterlife and so lives only for himself wakes up and discovers he is wrong, he has lost everything.

The wise man, therefore, does not ignore death. He prepares for it, and the best way to prepare for the journey into the dark is to go on that journey every day. This is what the religious romantic sets out to do. Through the practice of his religion, he sets out on the quest. He faces the dark. He meets with monsters. He tilts with windmills, draws his sword, engages in the battle, fights for the fair maiden, and defends the truth. How religion helps him do this is the subject of the rest of this book.

12

PAGANISM, POETRY, AND POINTERS

Why the Old Stories Matter

The Greeks told the tragic story of Orpheus, the son of the great god Apollo. Orpheus was the master of music, the prince of poetry, the one who gave the rites to the mortals for the practice of their religion. He fell in love with the beautiful Eurydice, who died after being bitten by vipers. Orpheus went on the long journey into the underworld to rescue his beloved, and he was able to charm Hades and Persephone, the king and queen of the realm of death. They allowed him to lead his beloved back to life on the provision that he would walk before her, never looking back until they reached the upper world. When he stepped out of the darkness, he looked back to see her, forgetting that he could not look back until they were both free, and so she vanished forever.

The curious and delightful thing about this story is that it is echoed in other myths in other cultures at other times around the world. The Japanese have a story of a husband named Izanagi who descends to the underworld to save his wife, Izanami. The Sumerian goddess Inanna goes down to conquer the underworld; the Nez Perce tell a story of Coyote, who does the same; and the theme of not looking back during an important rescue or adventure echoes in the stories of Lot's wife fleeing Sodom, Hansel and Gretel, and Jason's raising of Hekate.

The example can be multiplied countless times. The same stories with the same themes crop up time and again in one culture after another. Whether they are ancient myths, legends, folk tales, fantasy stories, or science-fiction and fantasy films, the same essential struggles occur in every age and among every people, and we delude ourselves if we think the fantastical stories of gods and goddesses intermingling with mortal men are the stuff of ancient cultures only.

The same stories live today in our comic books and movie theaters. There the superheroes do today what the gods did in ancient days. There ordinary newspaper reporters, students, and millionaires don masks and capes and spandex suits and so become great heroes. They fight villains who look and behave like demons. There, in the comic books and summer blockbuster movies, the barrier between the everyday world and the supernatural breaks down. Ordinary mortals assume supernatural powers. They become gods and engage in the battle between good and evil just as certainly and powerfully for us as the myths and mystery religions did for our ancestors so long ago.

What I find curious is that there is a type of human being who does not enjoy this very human activity. The cultural elite, the tasteful, and the academic either studies this phenomenon or ignores it, but it is more likely that he despises it. The literary critic looks down his fine nose at fantasy stories, science-fiction tales, and comic-book heroes, yet a vast majority of the population find such things not only entertaining but enlightening, and not only enlightening but enriching. They participate in the drama of the modern-day gods and goddesses in the comic book and on the silver screen with the gusto and enjoyment of a good religion.

The critics of superhero culture sneer that it is for boys in shorts. Those who despise fairy tales say they are interested not in fantasy but in facts; they are interested not in science fiction but in serious fiction. By this they mean they want to read novels about grown-ups committing adultery and then feeling guilty about it. From my perspective, there is nothing more childish and frivolous than grown-ups playing sex games, feeling guilty, and going to an analyst, and there is nothing more serious and eternal than the interplay of the gods and men. It may be that boys like comic books and girls like fairy tales and pimply teenagers like science fiction and tales of superheroes. I am on their side, and I am reminded that unless I become like these children, I cannot enter the kingdom, and it is their kingdom of kings and princes and knights and dragons and supermen and green goblins that I most want to enter. In comparison, adultery and angst and sex and psychoanalysis are terribly boring.

Myths, Magic, and Mystery

At the end of the last chapter I said that the second half of the book was about how the romantic religious person, through his religion, goes on the quest. Then I started this chapter by talking about pagan myths of redemption and release. Why begin with the ancient stories? Because the ancient tales wove religion and life together to show us that religion and life are meant to be woven together.

Myths (whether they are about ancient superheroes or comic-book superheroes) are not simply fanciful stories that are untrue; they are simple, fanciful stories that are very true. They are true even though they are not factual. A myth reveals truth through a fanciful tale. It does not do so like a fable, where a moral is tacked to the end of a fanciful story; nor does it do so like an allegory, where the characters represent certain truths. Instead, in a myth the truth is dressed up and acted out as in a drama. In a myth, truth and love and beauty put on masks and wear costumes and engage with lies and error and death and destruction. This is why superheroes do the same, because they are acting in a mythic manner.

*In a myth the truth is dressed up
and acted out as in a drama.*

Critics of the Christian religion will say that the whole thing is nothing but an amalgamation of pre-Christian myths. The dying and rising god, the hero-god born of a virgin, the gods become incarnate in human form—it was all there before Christian theologians thought it up. They say that Christians purloined the lot. "In fact," say the rationalist critics of Christianity, "their founder was just another ragtag preacher from a backwoods province of the Roman Empire. The idealistic nincompoop got caught up in some unfortunate political intrigue and was crucified for his mistake. Then the clever fellow Paul came along and began to make a god out of him, and his followers took the ball and ran with it. All sorts of myths, legends, mysterious rituals, and rites were swirling around the Roman empire, and the early Christians took a bit of that myth, a smidgen of this ritual, a pinch of that legend, a dash of this mystery religion, and mixed it all together with some ancient mumbo jumbo, a few miracle stories, and an atmosphere of mythic romance, and—hey, presto!— they came up with Christianity."

This fabricated story is then used to debunk Christianity as a fabricated story. With their theory that Christianity is just paganism warmed up, the scholars pretend to see through the whole Christian make-believe. There are several problems with their theory. First of all, congruence of time does not demand causation or even influence. In other words, just because two things occur at the same point in history does not necessarily mean that one caused the other or even influenced the other—even if it seems so. The two things that are similar might have other links deeper and more universal than what seem the obvious routes of influence. The fact that human beings worshipped the sun in Mexico, Egypt, and Australia doesn't necessarily mean that the civilizations in question influenced each other. The simpler answer is always to be preferred, and the less complex and conspiratorial conclusion is that worshipping the sun is simply a natural human activity.

If many different civilizations in the ancient Middle East developed indoor plumbing, it doesn't mean there was a mysterious link between the civilizations. It just means that human beings dislike the smell of sewage and therefore devise means of sanitation. It is the same with the supposed influence of the pagan religions on Christianity. Simply because certain ideas and customs developed at the same time and in the same place does not demand the influence of one culture on another.

Even if it can be shown that there was a cultural influence between Christianity and paganism, why should it be necessary that the Christians stole the ideas from the pagans? There is good evidence to show that the reverse is the case. For example, the Roman feast of Sol Invictus at the winter solstice was often thought to be the feast Christians copied to create Christmas. It now turns out that the celebration of Sol Invictus was developed after Christianity. S. E. Hijmans says there is no evidence of the Sol Invictus celebration predating Christianity, and Michael Anderson in *Symbols of Saints* gathers scholarly opinion that concludes there is no link between the date of Christmas and Sol Invictus. Some scholars therefore propose that the pagans (whose influence was waning) pumped up the Sol Invictus celebration to compete with the phenomenally successful new religion, which worshipped the rising Son of God—Christ Jesus. It is often thought that Christianity copied the Roman cult of Mithras. Both had a dying and rising god. Both had a form of ritual meal. Both had a form of baptism. They developed at the same time, but we needn't necessarily say that Christianity copied Mithraism. It is more likely that Mithraism copied Christianity. Indeed, the ancient Christian writers like Tertullian claimed that Mithraism was a foul imitation of Christianity, and all the writings of the period reveal that Christians regarded Mithraism as a demonic counterfeit and certainly not something to be imitated.

Even if one could prove the influence of paganism on Christianity, why would that necessarily be a bad thing? In fact, I would suspect a religion that did not connect its ritual and myth with the rest of the world's religions. Instead of invalidating the authenticity of Christianity, the connections validate it. The connections between paganism and Christianity do not show that Christians copied pagans, but that Christianity is part of a much larger, universal human religious context.

Myths and a Matrix of Meaning

If this is the case, then something else is going on in the rituals, mysteries, and myths of humanity, both in the ancient and modern worlds. If the same symbols and stories arise time and again throughout human culture, then we ought to conclude that these stories and symbols lie deep within the universal consciousness of humanity. If this is so, we are onto something truly remarkable. There seems to be a kind of symbolic religious literary code written into human experience. The matrix of meaning runs deep within the human heart, no matter where or when the person lives.

The themes of the overworld and underworld, the need for redemption and sacrifice, the story of the lost child, the hero's quest, the virgin mother, the dying redeemer, the rising god—all these are woven not just into the imagination of human beings but into their perception of everything in the world around them. The myths were linked with their own sufferings and fears and joys and sorrows, and also into the very fabric of the universe they perceived. The cycles of planting and harvest, the cosmic cycles of the sun, moon, and stars, the cycles of human conception and birth and living and dying were all woven together in the ancient stories. There was, in the human heart, some kind of poetry that saw meaning in everything and everyone, and this meaning was expressed in fantastic stories and myths and parables and poems.

The poems and parables and myths and stories all gave flesh to the deeper and more mysterious meanings that were otherwise difficult to unlock, and as the meaning was incarnated in the art, it hinted at a far deeper and more disturbing possibility that the meaning could one day be incarnated not only in art but in reality. If the stories enfleshed the meaning, then what if Meaning itself could be enfleshed? What if the story, which showed the truth, could really come true? What if the truth would be incarnated not just in a story but in history?

> *If the stories enfleshed the meaning, then what if Meaning itself could be enfleshed?*

This is the reality to which all the stories point: that the stories are accounts of truth being lived out in real life, just as piano music being played is the incarnation of the music in the score—and when you think about it, isn't this the dynamic and the glory of all art? That in some way the truths that were discussed discursively are shown to have life and breath and body and flesh? So a play comes to life with actors speaking the lines and emoting the passion. So a fictional story comes to life in a film or a play. So a painting reincarnates in oil or water and pigment and canvas and paper another reality, and that reality lives within that new incarnation of beauty, truth, and love.

A Myth Come True

If this is true, then all art and all stories and all cultures down through the ages at all times and in all places were striving and longing for a possibility that everyone knew would one day occur, but no one knew quite how. This possibility that all art and all stories and all architecture and myth and dance and drama point to is that Truth may one day be incarnate in one person who summarizes and epitomizes all truth.

This is why all the pagan stories repeated the same themes, used the same symbols, breathed the same air, felt the same emotions, and pointed to the same thing—because all the stories were springing from the depths of not just one storyteller, nor the depths of one culture or the history of one people, but of the history of humanity. The stories were all the same because they came from the same source: a source deeper and older than any one person or any one culture or any one history.

> *The stories were all the same*
> *because they came from the same*
> *source: a source deeper and older*
> *than any one person or any one*
> *culture or any one history.*

That source was, if you like, the "deeper magic from before the dawn of time."[1] The stories all echoed the same themes of lost children longing for home, of a hero who embarks on a quest to save his soul and save his people, of the sufferings of love and the pain of loss, of redemption through sacrifice, of the journey into the underworld to emerge victorious and save the beloved. Those themes and symbols and mythic emotions were universal because they were far more ancient and venerable than any one society or storyteller.

They were locked into the depths of the human heart because every human heart was longing for redemption, for sacrifice, and for love. Every human being was on a quest to conquer the underworld and save the beloved. Every human being was searching for redemption and release. This eternal human longing, unspecified down the long ages, was nevertheless expressed in a multitude of legends, myths, stories, poems, and parables as people poured out their longings to one another.

What they did not know was that within one people the truths they all held dear were being incarnated while they dreamed. Within one tribe in the ancient Middle East, the stories of sacrifice and redemption, of oppression and release, of death and life and love—all these themes were not being incarnated in beautiful stories about gods and goddesses. They were being enacted and fulfilled within the ordinary, dust-filled lives of just another nomadic tribe on the Arabian peninsula.

MIRACLES AND MAGIC
IN DUST AND DIRT

How the Hebrews Romanced Religion

As an English snob once said, "How odd of God to choose the Jews."[1] What is remarkable about the history of the Jewish people is that it is unremarkable. It is extraordinary because it is ordinary. In other words, the Hebrews did not build ziggurats and hanging gardens. They did not carve a mysterious and monstrous sphinx or construct pyramids that reflected the constellations' locations. They did not erect monolithic circles of stones, carve mysterious images across their desert plains, build an impossible city high in the Andes, or establish a civilization with gigantic deities enthroned as immortal kings and queens.

The Hebrews were shepherds. They were nomads in the no-man's-land of the Arabian desert. Their wandering is not wonderful, and the scene of their wandering is practically the only thing about them that causes me to wonder. Their desert was one of the most barren in the world. Their lives were simple and their customs sparse. The only other thing that is wonderful about them is their survival.

The Hebrews were just ordinary people trying to scratch out a living the best way they could. In this respect, their lives were like the lives of most ordinary people most of the time in most of the places of the world. Most ancient people, like most modern people, were not Egyptian pharaohs, Babylonian monarchs, Aztec princes, or Celtic chieftains and shamans. They were not even Wall Street bankers. The Hebrews were not members of the great civilizations. Wandering in the desert, they existed like the flotsam and jetsam of the ancient world. In fact, the Jews to this day recite, as a matter of pride, a verse from the Old Testament, "My father was a wandering Aramean."[2] Some scholars reckon that the name *Hebrew* comes from the word *'ivri*, which means "cross over" or "to be in transit," while others surmise that the word really comes from the Egyptian word *H'apiru*, which means "trash." In other words, the sophisticated Egyptians considered the wandering tribe to be "desert immigrant trash." How odd of God to choose the Jews.

> *What is remarkable about the history of the Jewish people is that it is unremarkable. It is extraordinary because it is ordinary.*

Mythical Mesopotamian Monotheists

In fact, the Hebrews are remarkable, but the reason they are remarkable is unpredictable and unexpected. They are remarkable because they epitomize the mythological. What I mean is that this tribe of Mesopotamian monotheists, these Jewish gypsies, these nomadic nobodies, this ragtag collection of "desert trash" captured in their history the spiritual and psychological history of the human race. They did so because they lived out, in an astounding way, all the great myths and legends of the world. The poignant tales of lost children, the transit through the underworld, the quest for redemption, the salvation from slavery, the passage from death to life, and the hero's battle with the forces of darkness—all these stories come alive in the ancient stories of the Hebrew people. The difference is, the stories are locked into history. The fantastic tales become family sagas.

The tales of mythological mystery and magic become mundane tribal legends. The superheroes are not so super. Instead of helmets, they wear turbans; their masks are scarves to shield their faces from the whipping sand of sandstorms; instead of capes, long woolen robes (except for the one who wore a coat of many colors). The Hebrews are not gods, but they talk and walk with God. They are not masters of hidden mysteries or astrologers. They are camel drivers, warriors, farmers, traders, and dwellers in tents.

Consider for a moment all the great mythic stories of the world. Think of their great themes. Each one can be found in the Old Testament, which is both the storybook and the history book of the Hebrew people. Are you looking for the story of the ordinary man who is really a prince, who hears the magic voice calling him to embark on a heroic quest? Has this ordinary hero a dark secret? Has he killed a man? Is he on a journey to reclaim his own soul as well as to overcome a powerful, dark lord and set his people free? It is the story of Moses.

Shall we tell the tale of the hero who must pass through the underworld to claim salvation? Does he go down deep into the darkest bowels of the earth? Does he face his own mortality, his own rebellion, his own weakness and poverty? Does he lose all to gain all? Does he sacrifice his own life, then rise victorious to save his friends and family and himself? Then remember Joseph, who was cast down into the pit, sold into slavery, and emerged triumphant as a ruler in Egypt. Or think of Jonah, the prophet who was thrown into the deep and dark chaos of the sea, swallowed by a great fish, only to be vomited out on the third day, soiled but triumphant. Remember Elijah, in the depth of the cave on the holy mountain, sitting and watching and waiting for the voice of God.

Do you long for a tale of the search for true love, for loyalty and bravery and courage in the face of the threatening dark? Does this love that overcomes all things point you to a greater love, and do those stories echo some greater universal truth? The stories are there in the Old Testament sagas of the love between Isaac and Rebecca, Jacob and Rachel, Boaz and Ruth. The same universal stories and themes that connect all humanity were lived out in the history of this ordinary, dusty tribe of nomads.

The same universal stories and themes that connect all humanity were lived out in the history of this ordinary, dusty tribe of nomads.

Ordinary Heroes

Are you one who loves the stories of heroes engaged in the battle against the seemingly indomitable forces of darkness? Shall the story have a supernatural dimension? Shall the hero be an underdog, an unlikely, ordinary boy who overcomes against great odds? Should there be a romantic interest? A battle not only for love but against lust? Then remember the story of Joshua, who went out to battle the people of Jericho, avoided the allure of Rahab, and won the victory through cunning and divine intervention. Do you love the story of the boy who is terrified of the giant but beats him and saves his family by outsmarting the huge oaf? Then remember David in his unlikely battle against Goliath. Don't forget the hero Samson, who fell for the beautiful woman—the femme fatale who proved to be his downfall—and how King David fell into the arms of another man's wife, then fell further into schemes of foul murder, betrayal, and revenge.

The fantastic stories of the interaction of the gods with men are also alive in the stories of the Old Testament. The difference is that the Old Testament stories present themselves as part of history. Do you like to hear about the gods coming down to earth? Remember the mysterious visit of three angels to Abraham, or Jacob's dream of the angels ascending and descending on a stairway to heaven. Remember Elijah taken up in the fiery chariot, or the angel walking in the fiery furnace with the three Hebrew boys.

In the myths and fantastical stories of the varied world cultures, the gods command the mortals. In the Hebrew stories, God the Creator speaks to his people in all manner of ordinary ways—through dreams, through night visions and morning terrors, through the words and works of ordinary life: a transcendental vision of a bush that seems to burn without being consumed; in the thunder, earthquake, wind, and fire; in a quiet voice to a boy serving in the temple at night; or in a still, small whisper at the entrance of the cave—the door to the underworld.

Not only are all the universal stories of the world enfleshed in the stories of the Hebrew people, but all the archetypal characters are there. In the great stories of the world, certain types of hero occur and recur, and in the Hebrew story they all appear not in fantastical forms but historical forms. The brave and handsome young warrior hero is the famous King David. The intelligent young hero who is orphaned and left alone to fend for himself in the desert is the patriarch Joseph. The princess who lies hidden and emerges as the brave hero of the story is Queen Esther. The beautiful bride, discovered at last by her handsome prince, is Rachel. The wise old man who mentors the hero is Eli to the boy Samuel, and Samuel to the boy David, and Elijah to the young Elisha.

> *Not only are all the universal stories*
> *of the world enfleshed in the stories*
> *of the Hebrew people, but all the*
> *archetypal characters are there.*

If all the heroes are there, so are all the villains. The murderous brother Cain, the rebel Jacob, the seductive Delilah, and the giant Goliath. Like any fanciful fairy tale, the cast list of the wicked kings and queens runs through the historical tapestry of the Old Testament like a dark burgundy thread: the Egyptian pharaoh, wicked King Ahab, evil Queen Jezebel, murderous Haman, jealous King Saul, and the weak royal Rehoboam.

Natural Miracles

"Come, now," you will say. "Your hypothesis is weak. The myths and stories of the world are fully of magic and sorcery and witches and monsters. This is fantastical fiction. Such things do not exist, and the same sorcery, magic, and wonder is in the Old Testament. Whales swallowing prophets? Paths opening in oceans? Talking snakes and magical bread from heaven? These marvelous magical elements show the Bible stories to be no different from the fairy stories. It is all make-believe."

It is a good point, and not only a good point but the point that reveals the important difference between the pagan stories and the Hebrew stories. To be sure, there is plenty of what seems like magic in the stories of the Old Testament, but there are two astounding differences. First, the miracles in the Old Testament are presented as historical events. The authors place their heroes in real time and in real places. The pagan myths and fairy tales may make reference to real places, but no one believed that the gods really lived on that particular mountain, or that Hanuman, the monkey god, moved a mountain from the Himalayas, or that the holy mountains are really the breasts of the great Earth Mother.

On the other hand, Father Abraham lived in the city of Ur of the Chaldees around 2000 BC, when there was a Babylonian empire in Mesopotamia, a great dynasty in Egypt, and a mysterious circle of stones being erected at Stonehenge. From that point on, the stories of the Hebrew people were locked into history, and as a result, the miracles that take place are portrayed as real historical events. What we make of those miracles is a different matter. We may try to explain them away with naturalistic explanations—"the burning bush was really a bush with flame-red foliage; the manna was an edible excretion from desert plants; the Red Sea that was parted was really the Reed Sea, a marsh Moses knew how to navigate"—or we may acknowledge each one as a supernatural intervention by the Almighty. How we explain the miracles is the subject of debate, but what is not debatable is that the Hebrews present the miraculous and marvelous not as fantastical fiction but as historical events.

The second curious thing about the miracles of the Old Testament, and what distinguishes them from magic, is that they are not only real but also natural. That is to say, while the miracles of the Old Testament are wonderful, they are not weird. They are interruptions, exaggerations, or exceptions to the normal action of the natural world, but they do not contradict the natural world. In the pagan stories, when Leda mates with a swan, or Daphne turns into a laurel, or Zeus becomes a cuckoo to seduce Hera, we are confronted with something definitely cuckoo. The pagan stories of amazing transmogrifications and monstrous magic are wonderful and whimsical, but they are also unnatural. That is because they are magic, and the magical always distorts what is natural, while the miraculous always fits in with what is natural.

For example, when the Red Sea parts, God is given the credit, but the miracle is accomplished through a natural cause: a mighty wind. The Hebrews are given bread from heaven, but stones are not magically transformed into bread. That would be magic, not a miracle. In the wilderness, they are given quails to eat, but nobody is turned into a quail. Even with the strange account of the Nile turning into blood, the miracle is not unnatural. Water changes into blood all the time. When I drink water, my body transforms some of it into blood. What would be unnatural is if the Nile were to be turned into a giant naiad who rose up to consume the enemy. My point is that the Old Testament miracles do not go against the laws of nature; instead they are unusual manifestations of what happens naturally.

The fact that the miracles are presented as real and natural events confirms and confounds the essential fact of the Old Testament. Hebrew stories really are a curious development in the history of the human race. On the one hand, they retell all the old stories with all the same characters and all the same themes. On the other hand, they lock the stories into history. We are expected to believe that the heroes are real. The events really happened. The pagans told stories of the gods and mortals interacting, but they were, if you like, stories that were pointing to a reality that was not yet a reality: that God and mortals could interact. Then along comes this nomadic tribe who claims that instead of many gods, there is one God, and that he really does interact with particular people.

Truth Coming into Focus

This God created the world, and he told Abraham to leave his tribe and country and set out for an unknown promised land. This Abraham was given a son, then told to sacrifice him, and then told not to. His son had sons, and their sons had sons, and the tribe was enslaved in Egypt. God called one of their number to lead them to the land that had been promised but still not discovered, and he delivered them from bondage, led them through the wilderness, and helped them get established in their new land. Gradually, through the Hebrew race, humanity's religious yearning is coming into focus: there is one God, not many, and the one God is active and involved in lives of particular people at particular times and particular places. This novelty is what theologians call "the scandal of particularity," for it is an incredible scandal that the transcendent creator of the universe should have an intimate relationship with anyone at all, but our eyes are opened with shock and delight at the quirkiness of the Almighty, who chose not only to have an intimate relationship with particular people, but with peculiar people: a nomadic tribe of "desert trash."

What was happening in the history of the human race is a development of religious consciousness. Humans first grunted at the moon, sun, and stars in awe; then they groveled at the deities they sensed were behind the power of the sun, moon, and stars.

Then they told stories about those wonderful beings and how they interacted with one another and the mortals on earth. Then this one dusty and hardheaded tribe of people had no time for such fanciful stories and far-fetched tales.

Instead of gods and goddesses flitting about and flirting about on amorous adventures, their God was dignified and determined. He was unknowable yet making himself known. He was at the same time out of this world yet down-to-earth. The Hebrew God had a job to do, and he was working with them right where they were, in the dust and dirt, the sun and sweat of the Middle East; there among the bleating goats, the spitting camels, the jealous brothers, spiteful wives, longing lovers, and wicked kings, there among the frightened and faithful mortals called the Jews, the God of all gods was working out a secret master plan.

14

OF GODS, GIRLS, AND GLORY

The Maiden and the Mystery

The expert storytellers tell us that there are only seven stories, and we keep telling them in many different forms. One of these stories is the tale of rags to riches, and a subset of the rags-to-riches story is the tale of Cinderella. In a Cinderella story, a humble, good, and beautiful orphan girl captures the heart of a handsome prince who, admiring not only her beauty but her goodness, marries her and sweeps her off to live happily ever after. The story is told in a multitude of ways in virtually every culture and in every time, from the ancient Greeks to modern Hollywood.

What is it about this story that so captures our imaginations? It undermines the powerful, haughty, and rich.

Invariably there are ugly sisters and a wicked stepmother who have all the money and contacts . . . and a hairdresser. They are brought low by Cinderella's lowliness. The girl herself is a virgin. She is poor, and she is pure. Not only is she pure but she is made of purity. She is honest and simple and young and free. We want our daughters to be like her. The handsome prince is wise as well as wonderful. This is how we wish all our young men were. In fact, the prince is like a god in his greatness. He comes down from the palace on high and takes the hand of the humble handmaiden. Her humility ennobles him, and his nobility humbles her. They condescend to each other. He magnifies her with his wealth and power. She magnifies him with her humility and grace.

Cinderella is given her nickname by her cruel sisters. It is a name of derision, for she is "cinders." She sweeps the floor. That's why she is lowly. She scrubs the grate, and that is why she is great. She mixes her tears with ashes. She is not only lowly; she is filthy. Cinders are ashes, and ashes are dust, and Cinderella is ashes to ashes and dust to dust. We love Cinderella because she is one of us. She is ordinary. She is hardworking. She is a woman of the earth and hearth. She is the earth mother and the hearth mother in the purest sense.

I have said that the Cinderella story is universal, but it takes different forms in different places for different people at different times. Think of the Hollywood movies that are Cinderella stories: *The Sound of Music* and *Pretty Woman* and *Maid in Manhattan* and *My Fair Lady* and *Annie* and *Working Girl* and the list goes on. These are our versions of the Cinderella story, but what interests me is that the ancients also told the Cinderella story, but with a disturbing and curious twist. They add a supernatural dimension; in their stories the girl is not swept off her feet by a powerful prince but by a powerful deity. The gods look down on human girls and are delighted. They do not waste their time with pumpkins turning into coaches, mice turning into footmen, and a glass slipper left behind. Instead they overwhelm and ravish their beauties. What is it about Zeus that makes him seduce? What is going on in these lascivious adventures? Why in so many cultures do the gods decide to mate with mortals?

As in all the stories, there is something more than meets the eye. The stories were not just ancient forms of pornography. When the gods met and mated with mortals, their actions pointed to something greater. They were pointing to a desired union between heaven and earth—between the invisible power of heaven and the visible beauty of earth. Their union was a union of the invulnerability of power with the vulnerability of beauty, and what could be more beautiful and more irresistible than a fair young maiden? There is more. The result of the unions were demigods—half-breeds who were human heroes because they had divine capabilities. When Zeus mated with Alcmena, and Hercules was produced, everything pointed to another event that would really happen in human history. When the human girls in the pagan stories produced heroic sons like Hercules, they were hinting at the hope that such a creature as a god-man might come true. The pagan stories were pointers and prophecies of the future.

The pagan stories were pointers and prophecies of the future.

A Divine Plan

God did not interact with the Hebrews simply for an interesting pastime. He had a plan, and the plan had order, mystery, majesty, and loveliness. Just as all the pagan heroic stories were played out in the dust and dirt of that unremarkable nomadic race, so this greatest myth of all was to be enacted in real time with real people in a real place. God's plan in playing out the human myths within the Hebrew history was a way of hiding himself within human history, and he hid himself within human history because eventually he planned to hide himself within a human being. The myths of gods mating with maidens gave the hint of how he would do this.

Of course, what I am referring to is the greatest Cinderella story of them all. The girl (like the girl in every Cinderella story) is a pure and innocent virgin. She is alone in the world. She is poor and lowly. Then the mysterious visitor comes. Not a fairy godmother but an angel named Gabriel. Her prince is not from the palace on the hill but from the palace beyond the heavens. The Blessed Virgin Mary accepts the word of love from God and becomes pregnant with his son. Here, the Christian says, is God come to earth. Here, through a miraculous marriage of heaven and earth, God takes human flesh and blood and steps into history. Here the God-Man is born as a little child.

"Stop!" I hear you cry. "You are admitting what the anthropologists and mythologists and teachers of comparative religion have said for ages, that the Christian myth of the incarnation is simply another fairy tale like all the ancient myths of old. It is simply the Christian version of the pagan myths!" You continue, "You are admitting that the clever Christians adopted and adapted the existing pagan ideas and applied them to their martyred hero, the tragic rabbi Jesus of Nazareth. He became the hero Hercules and his mother became Alcmene. In his rising and victory over the underworld, he stepped into the shoes of the ancient Egyptian god Osiris. You are admitting that the Christian stories and rituals were simply transferred wholesale from the old religion into the new."

So Washburn Hopkins writes,

The religions of the divine Mother and of Mithra had already taught the doctrine of a redeeming god, whose experience was shared by the initiated believer. Mortal man through the death and resurrection of the god became by partaking in the sacraments a partaker also in the divine nature; he was mystically cleansed of sin by blood or water and became a sharer in divine immortality. The epiphany of Dionysos became the epiphany of Christ.[1]

Because of the similarities between the ancient religions and Christianity, we are expected to dismiss Christian doctrine as no more than a human construction—a natural evolution of the religious mind, of no more real consequence than the development of indoor plumbing from an aqueduct. It seems so obvious—does it not?—that the Christian religion was a simple adaption of the existing pagan religions. I do not deny the similarity between the stories of Zeus and Alcmene and the annunciation of the angel Gabriel to the blessed Virgin Mary. Not only do I not deny the similarities, but I am delighted by them. It would be very suspicious indeed if the Christian beliefs did not connect with the beliefs of the religions that came before. I am not disturbed by similarities. What would disturb me is if the Christian beliefs were totally unconnected with what came before. Then I would suspect that someone had sat down to make them up out of his own mind.

> *What would disturb me is if the Christian beliefs were totally unconnected with what came before. Then I would suspect that someone had sat down to make them up out of his own mind.*

Checking the Facts

The similarities exist, and that is what makes the Christian beliefs so very fascinating; for once we admit the similarities, we must then go on and analyze the differences. If we are to avoid smug assumptions and sweeping statements, then we must not only examine the similarities between the ancient religions and Christianity but also see how they are different, and it is the differences, not the similarities, which are most remarkable.

First, we must consider the Hebrew setting in which the Christian beliefs were formulated. The idea that Jesus Christ was God, born by divine intervention to a virgin girl, was first recorded by Jews. Matthew, Mark, Luke, John, Peter, and their communities of faith came to believe in the idea of Jesus Christ the God-Man. What makes it unlikely that they simply adopted and adapted pagan ideas is that the surrounding pagan ideas were anathema to them. Already, the first Christians were struggling against the opposition of their fellow Jews, who considered them to be radical heretics and the members of a weird cult. Are we to believe that they would be so radical and revolutionary as to deliberately import pagan ideas and practices that ordinary, pious Jews would have considered the height of blasphemy? Hardly. We must find another answer for their idea that Jesus was the God-Man born of a simple virgin, and the only other reason we can find is that this truth was revealed to them by the God they trusted.

Because of the improbability that first-century Jews concocted the doctrine of the incarnation of God by stealing the idea from pagans, scholars have proposed that the first non-Jewish Christians grafted their ideas into the fledgling Jewish-Christian faith. They suppose that the pagan citizens of the Roman Empire added Christianity to their existing religions and eventually cross-fertilized their new religion with the old, adding ideas of god-men and virgin mothers to the previously pristine teachings of a wandering Jewish rabbi. Unfortunately the documentary evidence doesn't support the theory. The idea that Jesus of Nazareth was God in the flesh is present in the earliest writings of the New Testament, which were undoubtedly written by first-century Jews.

The second problem with the theory that the early Christians simply imported pagan ideas is that nowhere within paganism did they suppose that the gods were real historical people. Just as importing paganism into Judaism would have been anathema to the Jews, so the idea that the interaction of gods with men really happened in a village in Galilee would have been preposterous to the pagans. Furthermore, the stories of Judaism incarnated the ancient myths in historical ways—but unconsciously. The Jews never imagined that their own stories were pagan myths come true. The ancient myths were hidden within the historical stories of the Hebrew people in a natural and organic way. The myths were not imposed on the history as an afterthought, even though we can see what happened only in hindsight.

Finally, the early Christians themselves were in constant conflict with the pagan religions and died as martyrs in the conflict. If Christianity were simply the latest version of the pagan cults, why did Christians find the pagan cults so objectionable? If the divine Jesus Christ was simply another divine hero like the pagan heroes, then why not accept the divine emperor or the divine Hercules or participate in Mithraism? If the development of their religion was the wholesale acceptance of paganism, then why did the first Christians object to paganism so strenuously—even to the point of death?

The problem with the anthropologists' and comparative religionists' solution is not that it is obvious but that it is too obvious. They have made the mistake of assuming that similarities always imply influence, but certain strains within the human imagination, and especially within the human religious sensibilities, are simply universal aspects of being human. Because an Aborigine in Australia tells a story about the beautiful moon goddess, and an Inuit in Alaska does the same, does not mean that they have gotten together to share notes. Perhaps the truth is far simpler. They both tell stories about the beautiful moon goddess because the moon is beautiful and reminds them of a powerful and lovely lady.

The story of the blessed Virgin Mary accepting the Son

of God is related to all the pagan myths of gods and girls. It is related to all the Cinderella stories of poor girls swept off their feet by powerful masters, but it is related to these stories as the birth of a child is related to a schoolgirl's dreams of being a mother. The simple girl in Nazareth saying yes to God and receiving his Son within her own self is related to all the mystical and magical stories as the vague dreams and outlines of a story are within an author's mind before he writes. The pagan stories were whisperings of what was to come. They were glimpses of a future glory and shadowy hints of a plan that would become as particular as a pregnancy, as concrete as a crying child, and as human as the humble history of the whole Hebrew race. It was on this stupendous foundation that the rest of human history would be transformed.

The pagan stories were whisperings of what was to come. They were glimpses of a future glory and shadowy hints of a plan that would become as particular as a pregnancy, as concrete as a crying child.

15

SUPERMAN OR SON OF MAN?

The Man and the Mystery

I was almost thirty years old before I realized that my idea of Jesus Christ was that he was a kind of first-century Superman. Instead of the mild-mannered Clark Kent, it was the mild-mannered carpenter from Nazareth. Jesus didn't step into a phone booth and change into a red-and-blue costume; he stepped off the beach to walk on the waves. He didn't leap tall buildings with a single bound, but he did levitate and radiate with two other superheroes, called Moses and Elijah, and when it was all over, he flew back to heaven. Jesus didn't fight for "Truth, Justice, and the American Way," but he did call himself the Truth, the Life, and the Way. Superman came from a different planet, named Krypton. Jesus came from a different world, called heaven.

It was easy to believe that Jesus Christ, with his supernatural powers, was like Superman long ago and far away.
Consequently, it is easy to write the Jesus story off as a comic
book from the first century. We made up fantastic stories
about Superman. They made up stories about their own superman. We got a comic-book hero. They got a cosmic hero. So
what? They're both fascinating and fantastical stories, if you
like that sort of thing. The intellectual will pull on his pipe and
say, "We see in both stories the endless and rather charming
capacity of simple human beings to make myths that convey
their highest dreams and aspirations"—thoughtful look up
through the tobacco smoke; takes off spectacles and wipes
them slowly—"and isn't it really rather beautiful to think that
perhaps in some sort of way these stories—so quaint and so
childish—might be communicators of truths and values for
those who hold them dear?"

Uh-huh. So the story of Jesus Christ being God in human
form—that's all just a myth, right? Right and wrong. The story
works on us as all the other myths do—in a mysterious and
wonderful way—with the big difference being that Christians
believe it is true. That's right. Not simply "true" in a meaning-
ful way, but true in a historical way. It was actual and factual.
In other words, the story of Jesus being God incarnate and
being born of a virgin is like the other myths from Hercules
to Superman, except that it really happened.

Here is the turning point of this book, and the turning
point of history, and the turning point (if we allow) of our
lives. So far this book has been full of romance. Like romance,
it has been whimsical, wild, and even witless. I have waxed
lyrical about stories and theories and ideas and ideals. Now

we have come to something solid and real and historical and factual that we must reckon with. We must come face-to-face with the person of Jesus of Nazareth and make a decision. Like Pontius Pilate, we sit before this mysterious man from Nazareth, and we must try to figure out who on earth he is.

> *Like Pontius Pilate, we sit before this mysterious man from Nazareth, and we must try to figure out who on earth he is.*

Anyone who thinks Jesus of Nazareth is not a man of mystery clearly knows very little about him. One reading of a gospel straight through will correct the misapprehension. That Jesus Christ is such a mystery to us is because, from the very beginning, his disciples made enormously outrageous claims about him. From the beginning of Christianity the followers of Jesus of Nazareth said, "He is the Son of God. He is the creative force of the universe. He is the source and ending of all things. He is the Savior of mankind, the Redeemer, the Eternal Shepherd, the King of the Cosmos." The claims and titles go on and on, and from the beginning Christians have spoken eloquently about their beliefs about Jesus, and anyone who wishes at all to take life seriously must consider these claims.

To put it bluntly, the claims that Christians make for Jesus of Nazareth seem to clash with the surface facts about his life. Those who have no faith say, "Pshaw. Come now. What is all this talk about Son of God, the Alpha and the Omega, the one by whom all things were created and hold together? What is this cosmic Christ, this incarnate God, this supernatural being? It is hogwash. Wishful thinking. Fairy tales fabricated by fanatics. Jesus of Nazareth himself never claimed to be an incarnate god. Such a thought would be anathema to a good first-century Jewish rabbi. We know that he was merely a good religious teacher—one of many—a miracle worker of sorts, an itinerant gospel preacher with a ragtag bunch of country bumpkins in tow. The poor man was in over his head. He got caught up in the political hurly-burly of the day. Perhaps he even believed the exalted claims his followers made for him. He was swept along by the fever pitch of excitement and wound up getting himself crucified. Then, long after he died, the apostle Paul had some sort of psychotic experience and started to pump up this preacher into an incarnate deity, a cosmic Christ, a Savior of the world, and the Great Judge who would come at the end of time. He took his tragic death and turned it into a theological drama, lifting ideas wholesale from existing pagan religions. A happy coincidence of history and cultural shifts allowed this great new story to grow and become popular, and after a few hundred years, the Emperor Constantine himself swallowed the beautiful tale (or saw the political advantage of the new religion), and the rest, as they say, is history."

Fact and Fiction

Now, this version of the story seems so much more rational, and those who trouble themselves to give the subject the most

shallow consideration and read a few books by modern scholars on the subject will trot away having happily swallowed the
propaganda. Consequently they now regard Jesus as a sort of
proto-Gandhi—a sincere holy man who got in too deep and
paid the price. They admire Jesus of Nazareth as they might
admire Martin Luther King Jr. or some other sage or martyr for
a cause. The problem is, the modern scholar's approach (which
calls the traditional Christian version a fantastic myth) is itself
an unbelievable fabrication. It is a seemingly easy solution to
the mystery, but like most easy solutions to mysteries, it is an
incorrect solution. The one who solves mysteries with easy
solutions has usually jumped to conclusions, believed theories
instead of evidence, and exaggerated clues while ignoring facts.

Like any good detective, we have to get past the easy solutions. The easy solution may be a sincere misunderstanding,
a frame-up, or an intentionally fabricated illusion in order to
deflect the detective's persistent and troublesome questions.
The facts of the matter simply do not match up with the modern scholar's easy but false conclusion.

The first problem with their version of the significance of
Jesus of Nazareth is their sense of timing. They would have us
believe that all the talk of Jesus of Nazareth being an incarnate
Son of God, the cosmic Christ, the one by whom all things
were created, and the dreadful Judge of mankind, was a fantastic theological invention, cooked up much later by the Christian
church, and that nobody really believed all that "Cosmic Christ,
Son of God, Redeemer" stuff in the early days.

The trouble with this theory is that this is exactly what
the early Christians did believe about Christ in the early days.
We have a document called the New Testament, which even

by the most liberal methods of dating (based on textual criticism, documentary evidence, and archaeology) must have been completed by the mid-90s of the first century. That is only sixty years after the death of Jesus of Nazareth. The scholars would have us believe that it was a long expanse of time before all the mythical and magical stuff about Jesus being the Cosmic Christ evolved in the minds of his followers. This is simply a lie. It was only sixty years.

Think for a moment about our own lives. What happened sixty years ago? I am writing in the year 2013. Sixty years ago was the year 1953. I was born in 1956. My parents were born in 1927. My mother is still alive. Many people are alive today who remember the 1950s. This means that by the time the New Testament was completed, there were still plenty of people living who remembered the events. A man who was twenty when Jesus Christ walked the earth would have been eighty by the time all scholars admit the New Testament was completed.

However, it's not as extreme as that. We know that Saint Peter and Saint Paul died in the persecutions of Christians by Nero in the year 65. This means all of Paul's and Peter's writings in the New Testament were completed before that date. Also, the New Testament book the Acts of the Apostles recorded the lives and ministries of Peter and Paul. It does not record their deaths, but surely if they had died martyrs' deaths by the time it was written, the author would have recorded this tragic event. Since Peter and Paul died in the year AD 65, we can conclude that the Acts of the Apostles was written before that date. Furthermore, the Acts of the Apostles is the companion volume to Saint Luke's gospel. They were written by the same person. This means Luke's gospel was also composed before AD 65. In addition, Luke's gospel was probably dependent on Mark's gospel—which means that the gospel of Mark also must have been written only thirty years after the death of Jesus Christ.

This means that the majority of the New Testament was completed, not by the year 95 as some suggest, but thirty years earlier. The "great long time span" in which fanciful doctrines about Jesus of Nazareth evolved among the Christian community was, at the very most, only sixty years, and that has now been halved. Eyewitnesses of the events were still living. Those who knew Jesus of Nazareth, and knew who he believed himself to be, were there to correct any wrong teaching. How likely is it that Paul and Peter and the others who preached such outrageous things about the wandering rabbi from Nazareth would have been believed if what they said contradicted what Jesus himself taught? The people who heard them preach had known Jesus himself.

How likely is it that Paul and Peter and the others who preached such outrageous things about the wandering rabbi from Nazareth would have been believed if what they said contradicted what Jesus himself taught?

Set the Record Straight

What did Peter and Paul think and write about Jesus of Nazareth in those first thirty years after his death? In writing to the first Christians in the city of Colossae, Paul said of Jesus Christ,

> [He] is the image of the invisible God, the firstborn over all creation. For in him all things were created: things in heaven and on earth, visible and invisible, whether thrones or powers or rulers or authorities; all things have been created through him and for him. He is before all things, and in him all things hold together.[1]

To the Christians in the city of Galatia he wrote: "When the fullness of time had come, God sent forth his Son, born of woman."[2] These are not words taken out of context. They are not scraps of fanciful thinking, but an astounding, complete, and comprehensive philosophy and theology built on a belief that Jesus of Nazareth really was the Son of God. The entire New Testament is consistent in its teaching that Christ is the incarnate Son of God.

The entire New Testament is consistent in its teaching that Christ is the incarnate Son of God.

Not long after Peter and Paul, the apostle John used the language of Greek philosophy to say that Christ is the "Word"—the divine energy source of creation. So he wrote,

> In the beginning was the Word, and the Word was with God, and the Word was God. . . . Without him nothing was

made that has been made. . . . And [he] made his dwelling among us. We have seen his glory, the glory as of the one and only Son, who came from the Father, full of grace and truth.[3]

These are not isolated ideas. The New Testament echoes with the same cosmic claims that Jesus of Nazareth is the turning point of history, the Redeemer of the world, the Savior of mankind.

Still the scholars will insist that Jesus of Nazareth never had such grandiose ideas about himself, but again, they misread the accounts in the Gospels and miss the whole point. One of the points they miss is that Jesus of Nazareth was teaching and acting within the Jewish prophetic tradition, and that tradition considered actions to speak louder than words. Jesus proclaimed his divinity quite clearly—especially at his trial—but more importantly, he proclaimed his self-understanding as the Son of God through his striking and prophetic actions. To understand these actions we need to understand the Old Testament imagery and stories they reference.

To reveal that he was God in human form, time after time Jesus did what God did in the Old Testament. For example, when Jesus fed the five thousand in the wilderness and gave them "bread from heaven," he was doing what God the Father did with the Hebrews in the wilderness when he fed them manna, or "bread from heaven." In other words, through his actions, Jesus was showing himself to be God the Father come again.

Another example is his saying, "I am the Good Shepherd."[4] All through the Old Testament the image of the shepherd is vital and real for the Hebrew people. The prophet Ezekiel said that God himself will come and shepherd his people. God himself will come and be the Good Shepherd.[5] When Jesus called himself the Good Shepherd, he was not saying he was a very nice fellow who was fond of sweet little lambkins. All his hearers would have understood what we miss: when Jesus called himself the Good Shepherd, he was equating himself with God. When he calmed the storm and walked on the waves, he was fulfilling the Old Testament imagery about God being the one who has power over the waters at creation and at the crossing of the Red Sea, and who the writer of Job says "walks on the waves of the sea."[6] These are only a few examples of the way, time and again throughout the events of his life, Jesus revealed through powerful words and works that he understood himself to be the Son of God.

> *All his hearers would have understood*
> *what we miss: when Jesus called*
> *himself the Good Shepherd, he*
> *was equating himself with God.*

So What?

The evidence demands a verdict. Everyone who has stopped to consider the claims of Jesus Christ must make a decision. Is he who he says he is, and who his followers believe him to be? The choice is very simple and very stark. He is either a good religious teacher or the Son of God. We've seen that his followers from the very beginning have believed him to be the Son of God, and we've seen that he understood himself to be the Son of God. These facts force us to render a verdict. C. S. Lewis famously stated,

A man who was merely a man and said the sort of things Jesus said would not be a great moral teacher. He would either be a lunatic—on a level with the man who says he is a poached egg—or else he would be the Devil of Hell. You must make your choice. Either this man was, and is, the Son of God: or else a madman or something worse. You can shut Him up for a fool, you can spit at Him and kill Him as a demon; or you can fall at His feet and call Him Lord and God. But let us not come with any patronising nonsense about His being a great human teacher. He has not left that open to us. He did not intend to.[7]

So, for the sake of argument, let us say that we have come to the grudging conclusion that this man is who he says he is: he is the Son of God. He is God in human form. He is the Alpha and the Omega, the beginning and the end. He is the Judge of all humanity. He is the fount of all life. He is the Way, the Truth, the Life. As God made Man, he is the bridge between humanity and God. Let us say that we nod our heads and follow the magic and logic of it all and admit the truth. We still have to ask, "So what?" This is where the romance of religion comes in, for we do not want to respond to such a stupendous truth with mere logic alone. We do not want to simply accept a dogma when we can accept a transformation.

*We do not want to simply
accept a dogma when we can
accept a transformation.*

Our response to this truth must be one of wonder and awe and delight and fear at where it will lead us. If Jesus Christ is God in human form, then human history is terrifyingly transformed. This is not simply a bit of historical trivia. It is not a paranormal oddity, as if the existence of leprechauns had suddenly been proven. This is an actuality that changed history forever. The facts are there. The Christian church still exists and is growing. Billions still follow this man they claim is the Son of God.

If this is true, then it is the central truth of human history; it must be accounted for. Billions testify that this is not just a truth; it is a way and a life. That is to say, it is not just a historical fact to be believed; it is a way to be walked and a life to be lived. The awesome acceptance of this reality shocks the system. A paradigm shift happens; an earthquake in our understanding takes place. This fact changes everything. There is a transformation and a transaction, and the mystery of this transformation and transaction into a new life is bound up in the further mystery not only of who Jesus of Nazareth was but why he died and what that means.

16

THE SACRED SACRIFICE

On Death, Redemption, and Romantic Heroes

There is a moment in Mel Gibson's gory movie master-piece *Apocalypto* when you suddenly understand what the whole pagan human sacrifice thing is about. The hero has been captured by the bloodthirsty Mayans and hauled to the top of a pyramid with his friends. The captives are painted bright blue. One by one they are forced to the edge of the pyramid to have their hearts cut out and held up to the gods while still beating. Then they are beheaded, and the heads tumble down while the blood gushes. Suddenly you gasp and you get it: they want to please the angry sky god. So they give him the most precious thing they have: human life. They know that human life ends when the blood gushes out, so they paint them blue like the sky, and shed lots of blood to make the sky god happy. When the sky god is happy, he will give them sunshine and rain when they need it to make their crops grow. He will also give them the power they need to defeat their enemies. That's the point of sacrifice for primitive pagans. It's scary. It's gory. But given their worldview, there's a certain logic to it.

There's also a certain logic in the way a different understanding about sacrifice developed among the Jews. All around them in the Middle East four thousand years ago, the people were pulling out the hearts of their maidens, decapitating their young men, and chucking their kiddies alive into fiery furnaces to please their terrible gods. The Jews sacrificed goats and sheep and oxen and pigeons instead. Was it the same thing? You would have thought so. However, when you read the Old Testament, you discover that the Jews made sacrifices to their God for other reasons. First of all, they sacrificed animals instead of people because they believed human sacrifice was not demanded by their God. Their sacrifices were offerings to thank God for the good things they had and to ask forgiveness for the wrong things they'd done. In other words, their religion had a moral dimension that the pagan religions lacked. The Jewish religious ritual of offering God one of their animals sealed the deal—just as they might have sealed a peace treaty with a neighboring warlord by giving him ten sheep or goats.

There was another aspect to their understanding of animal sacrifice that was different from the usual pagan understanding shown in *Apocalypto*. When the Jews were about to escape from slavery in Egypt, they were told that the "angel of death" would pass over each house and the eldest son in each household would die. However, if they slaughtered a young lamb and spread his blood over their front door, their oldest son would be spared. In other words, the lamb would be a substitution for their son. A transaction would be completed and a deal sealed. The Jews celebrated this event every spring, and they still do. It's called Passover, and the lamb they slaughter is called "the Lamb of God."

Love and Death

All of this Jewish background explains how the first Christians (who were Jews) came to understand the death of Christ. Lest anyone step in and say, "All this talk about the blood of Jesus Christ and his sacrificial death? It's all just brutal, bloodthirsty, primitive, pagan religion warmed up. How can anybody believe such horrible, superstitious nonsense in this day and age where we have iPads and Facebook and toilets that flush?" The first Christians didn't explain Jesus' death as a sacrifice to conform to pagan religion. They explained it as the antidote to pagan religion. Jesus' death was not a gory death to satisfy a bloodthirsty monster sky god. Instead, Jesus was the Lamb of God—the one who voluntarily took death for somebody else and, in taking the punishment, forgave them. This self-sacrifice was seen as something to give thanks for, and so the first Christians (like the Jews at Passover) commemorated the sacrifice in a ritual called *Eucharist*, which is Greek for "thanksgiving."

> *The first Christians didn't explain Jesus' death as a sacrifice to conform to pagan religion. They explained it as the antidote to pagan religion.*

All of this talk of bloodshed and gore and sacrifice, however, still makes some modern Christians squeamish, despite the fact that they have no problem ordering a rib-eye steak. They think modern people won't like or can't understand ideas like sacrifice, so they skirt around it and put about the theory that Jesus Christ's death was really something else. They suggest that he simply died as a martyr for a noble cause and that for many years after his tragic death, he was remembered as a noble and glorious martyr. After all, one can buy T-shirts bearing the profile of Che Guevara, watch the film *Gandhi*, and celebrate Martin Luther King Jr.'s birthday—all in celebration of the nobility and courage of one who gave his life for a cause in which he believed.

The problem with this is that we must deal with a certain little difficulty called the New Testament. This document, if it is anything at all, is an accurate record of what the Christians in the first six decades after the death of Jesus Christ believed about the one they called their Lord. It is easy enough to believe that Jesus Christ was simply a martyr for a new belief or a political movement, but the New Testament doesn't offer that version of events. Not nowhere. Not nohow.

The first Christians didn't believe Jesus Christ to be merely a martyr for a cause. They believed him to be the second

Adam—the representative man—the man who stood in for the whole of humanity. They taught that Jesus Christ had died for them and died that they might live.[1] They believed that through his death their sins were forgiven and that through his death they could have eternal life. Now, where on earth might they have gotten such preposterous ideas? How could they believe such a thing? And even more mind-boggling—how could people in the twenty-first century attempt to believe such arcane and incomprehensible religious statements?

For yes indeed, travel down the highways of America today and you will see billboards that declare, "Jesus Saves"—and they are not advertisements for the local bank. You will see signs that shout out, "Jesus died to save you from your sins!" Tune in to the local gospel station to hear a backwoods preacher affirm that you must "accept Jesus into your heart and believe that he died for you and get saved." What on earth does it all mean? And how could the death of a wandering rabbi two thousand years ago possibly have an effect on me here today with my iPhone, my latte, and my three-car garage?

The Rise of the Romantic Hero

This is where the romantic heroes of all the movies and myths and stories suddenly step back onstage. The great heroes all bear a wound. The wound is their fatal flaw, their weakness, their Achilles' heel. This weakness is built in so that the audience will identify with the hero, and when we say *identify* we do not simply mean "like him" or even "feel sorry for him" or "be sympathetic." The scriptwriter, mythmaker, and movie director is trying to do much more than that. He is attempting to get the members of the audience to identify so deeply with the hero that they embark on a personal emotional journey with him. They step into his shoes. They step into his skin. They live out his life. They go on his adventure with him and become one with him for a couple of hours. The success of this mysterious transaction is ultimately the success or failure of the myth or the movie.

It is a poor analogy, perhaps, and the pious will be dismayed at my comparison of Jesus Christ to a mythical movie hero, but the connection is not without merit. Like all analogies, it is limited and faulty, but like all analogies, it points the way to a deeper truth, and the deeper truth is that Christianity involves a transaction like this, but one that is much more profound and existentially magnificent. The reason Christians insist that "Jesus Christ died to save you from your sins" is because they have experienced freedom from the darkest side of their nature through a mysterious identification with Jesus Christ. They insist that they have been "healed by his wounds" and "saved by the precious blood of the Lamb" and "redeemed by the cross of Christ." At this point the most important thing to try to imagine is that they are not teaching a theological theory or proposing an abstract doctrine. They are trying to explain an existential experience. They are attempting to explain a mystery, and a mystery is something that can be experienced even if it cannot be explained.

Like a person in love, the Christian is trying to put into words not what he believes but what he has experienced. So he struggles for expression. He says, "I was baptized into Christ's death and resurrection." Or, "I have put on Christ." Or, "I have died with Christ and now I live in Christ." Or, "I no longer live but Christ lives in me." A person who has not experienced this cannot understand it any more than a person who has never been in love can understand the experience of love.

> *Like a person in love, the Christian is trying to put into words not what he believes but what he has experienced.*

What is required when faced with these claims is not an incredulous sneer but a conscious and inquisitive curiosity. "Billions of people claim to have had this experience. Can such incomprehensible claims possibly be true? If so, how might they be true?"

At this point, the religious romantic points his nose in the air, adjusts the tilt of his hat, and says, "But of course these claims are true! They are not only true; they are beautiful. And they are not only beautiful, but they are good! They are as beautiful and true and good as a sleeping child or a morning in May. They are as beautiful and good and true as the sweet love of a maiden or the pure idealism of a dashing youth. They are as beautiful, true, and good as the noblest symphony, the most poignant song, the most tragic of dramas, and the sweetest of poems." The romantic hero continues his challenge, "Cynic! Will you sneer at love? Forsooth, will you trample on all that is noblest and finest and good and true? Take your sword from its scabbard, knave, for I must defend the fair maiden called Love!"

For in this interaction between the suffering Christ and the one for whom he died, we witness not a theological theory or an ecclesial construct but a transaction of trust, a covenant of life, and a consummation of love. To put it very simply, the human soul, longing for salvation in this dark vale of tears, sees in the dying and rising God the source of forgiveness and love and life. They open their hearts to this existential reality and join their whole beings with what they perceive as the everlasting source of life and love. An invisible transaction takes place. Their darkness, doubt, fear, and loss are exchanged for light, certainty, love, and life. This transaction is what we call faith. It is, in its first instance, a gift from God to the human soul, and in receiving it, the human soul finds life.

> *In this interaction between the suffering Christ and the one for whom he died, we witness not a theological theory or an ecclesial construct but a transaction of trust, a covenant of life, and a consummation of love.*

At this point the theories about what really happened on a certain dark Friday afternoon outside Jerusalem are just that—mere theories. They may illuminate the mysterious transaction, but they do not explain it. The theologians may write books about it as the psychologists may write books about love, but the result will be dry, predictable, wordy, and dull. Much better are the witnesses of the saints; like the poet's witness to love, the saint speaks of the transaction and the transformation that has taken place.

The saints offer us not an explanation but a description. They speak of release and redemption. They speak of forgiveness and healing. They say they are "born again"—that they have known the "dart of longing love."[2] They have been "baptized in the Spirit." They have been "purified by the Holy Fire." Like the language of love, their mystical words are immediately recognized and understood by others who have had the same experience, but for those on the outside, it remains terrifying and incomprehensible at worst, and at best an arcane and abstract theological theory.

At the heart of their experience of redemption is a new dimension of life. They feel that they have begun to live life "more abundantly." This brings us, therefore, not only to the death of Jesus Christ, but to what came next, for Christians say that his death would have only been a martyr's death if it ended there. However, it did not end there, for the real turning point came three days later. Christians insist that Jesus Christ died but he did not stay dead. He rose. He came back to life, and he lives still; and that has made all the difference.

THE ROAD
LEADS
EVER ON

CONSPIRACY, HEARSAY, AND HISTORY

The Event That Changed Everything

I have to admit that I'm a sucker for conspiracy theories. The more outrageous they are, the better. The idea that shadowy forces within the United States government engineered the attack on their own country on September 11 stirs and disturbs me. I'm intrigued by the proposal that John F. Kennedy was killed by the Mafia, that his brother was killed by an assassin programmed by the CIA, that Queen Elizabeth I was really a man, that Jimmy Carter is one of old Joe Kennedy's boys, and that Bill Clinton is a Rockefeller love child. I'm fascinated by the theory that Princess Diana was murdered by the Duke of Edinburgh, that Elvis is still alive, and that it was George Bush Sr. who was really behind the plot to assassinate Ronald Reagan. It's exciting to imagine that a cabal of secret forces are about to usher in a one-world government, that the English royal family are reptilian shape-shifters, and that Adolf Hitler is still alive on a top-secret military base on the moon.

I'm intrigued by conspiracy theories, not because I think they are true but because they are amusing and because they reveal a curious quirk in human nature. There is a kink in the human mind that draws us into an unreal world where obvious facts become evidence not for reality but for a clever cover-up of reality. In this fantasy world nothing is what it seems to be. The conspiracy theorist begins with a theory and a conspiracy, and forces all the facts to fit. What you see is not what you get, and what you get is not what you see. Everything is an illusion; the existing evidence becomes a clear proof of the opposite of what it seems to prove, and the lack of evidence just shows how good the cover-up really was. "Of course there is no evidence that the Queen of England is a reptilian alien!" cries the conspiracy theorist. "That just goes to show how professional her government is at silencing witnesses and covering up the truth, and isn't that sort of secrecy and deception exactly what you'd expect from a reptilian shape-shifter??!!"

Should you dare to disagree with the conspiracy theorist, you only confirm his wild belief that he is a lone prophet in the wilderness—one of the few who know the "real truth"— and that everyone else is blinded by the clever lies of the mainstream media, the one-world government, and a vast conspiracy between the Jews, the Freemasons, the vegetarians, the Illuminati, the guys who put fluoride in our drinking water, and the people who wear Birkenstocks.

What I find even more amusing and intriguing is that the same mentality that regards evidence as an obvious fabrication and lack of evidence as proof of a cover-up is commonplace among the intelligentsia who normally snigger at those poor souls who cling to their conspiracy theories. When it comes to the death and resurrection of Jesus Christ, the normally hard-headed and rational nonbeliever suddenly becomes as wide-eyed and wild as the craziest conspiracy theorist. Faced with the evidence for the resurrection of Christ, like any conspiracy theorist, the scholar believes that the "evidence" is faked. Then he comes up with a theory for "what really happened" and makes all the facts fit—even if real evidence has to be ignored, dates twisted, witnesses discredited, documents ignored, facts forced into fiction, and extravagant theories of government cover-ups fabricated out of thin air.

> *When it comes to the death and resurrection of Jesus Christ, the normally hard-headed and rational nonbeliever suddenly becomes as wide-eyed and wild as the craziest conspiracy theorist.*

Here we have the most revolutionary and radical hypothesis of history: the Christians claim that the Jewish prophet Jesus of Nazareth rose from the dead. Physically. However, before he could rise from the dead, he had to have really died. So the Christians point out that Jesus really did die on that dark Friday afternoon. They recount how he was flogged to within an inch of his life and then finished off by professional executioners.

Not only were the executioners professionals, but their careers and even their lives depended on them doing a thorough job. Furthermore, this execution took place in public in front of a howling crowd, who was there to make sure the job was done properly. That Jesus of Nazareth was killed around AD 30 outside Jerusalem by a cohort of Roman soldiers is a fact that even the most hard-hearted atheist historian accepts as one of the best-documented events of ancient history.

Nevertheless, intelligent men who are otherwise happy and sane suddenly start furrowing their brows, foaming slightly at the mouth, and devising far-out conspiracy theories about the death of Jesus of Nazareth. It cannot be that he rose from the dead, for (according to their assumptions) that simply can't happen. Therefore, it must be that he wasn't dead to start with.

So without any evidence—documentary, witnesses, archeological, historical, or otherwise—they suppose that it wasn't really Jesus who died. It was somebody else. Maybe it was his brother James, who looked like him, or Judas Iscariot, or a Jesus lookalike the disciples used to give the real Jesus a break from the rigors of celebrity life. While the mysterious lookalike was crucified, Jesus slipped off quietly to Tibet or Africa or India, where he was educated by swamis or gurus, or he simply started a nice life in Provence, sipping wine and lounging on the patio, watching his girlfriend, Mary

Magdalene, play with their kids, who would eventually become Merovingian kings.

Other, more lofty-minded theorists say that Jesus Christ was only a spirit being anyway, and it was only his body that died on the cross, and so his body was just an illusion. It was not real. Therefore his death was not death; it was only him throwing away a bit of trashy material stuff so he could emerge as the spirit being he always was. And this from people who find the supernatural answer that he rose from the dead too hard to believe?

We now come to those who tell us with a straight face that Jesus didn't really die on the cross because they gave him drugged wine and he just passed out. Or maybe he passed out from the intense pain. Either way, he woke up again a few days later and everyone thought he had risen from the dead.

Let's get this straight: the man was flogged with leather straps that had bits of metal, pottery shards, and glass tied into them. This fiendish flogging ripped great chunks of flesh from his body. He was beaten to within inches of his life because Pontius Pilate wanted to punish him but not crucify him. Then Pilate changed his mind and decided to crucify him anyway. After dragging the heavy cross through the city streets, Jesus was nailed to it by professional executioners who, instead of breaking his legs to hasten his death, stabbed him through the heart with a spear.

Nevertheless, someone slipped past the professional execution squad to give Jesus drugged wine. Would that have been one of his followers—all but one of whom fled in terror when he was taken? Maybe it was one of the professional executioners, who suddenly went all soft and risked his own life to give the criminal an overdose of painkiller? The story includes that detail, but it also includes the detail that Jesus refused the anesthetic.

Let us imagine for a moment that such a preposterous conspiracy theory is true, and Jesus somehow survived the crucifixion. Now we must believe that Jesus woke up in a freezing-cold tomb on a chilly morning in April, having suffered scourging, crucifixion, massive blood loss, shock, and a spear wound to the heart. First he unwrapped the shroud and burial wrappings and took care to fold them neatly at the foot of his bed. Then (from the inside) he rolled back a stone on the outside of the tomb that weighed a couple of tons.

He then stumbled out, totally naked, and limped up to the disciples on his bloody feet—his back was still raw meat, and his head was covered with puncture wounds and contusions. He showed them his hands and gasped out a greeting between the stabs of agonizing pain from the spear wound. Most people would have concluded that Jesus had somehow survived crucifixion and given him first aid and put him to bed. The disciples, however, said, "How wonderful! Something that has never happened before has happened! The Lord of Life has risen from the dead! Let's write it all down and start a new religion!"

This brings us to the next category of conspiracy theorists. This group of resurrection deniers says that Jesus of Nazareth really did die, but his body went missing, so his disciples started to believe what they wished was true: that their friend had risen from the dead.

What happened to Jesus' corpse is only limited by the imagination of these conspiracy theorists, who must find another answer for the claim of the resurrection. One scholar supposes that Jesus' body disappeared because it was abandoned or hurriedly buried in a shallow grave, and the dogs ate it. Never mind the historical evidence that the Jews were required to bury their dead respectfully or the documentary evidence that the body was buried in a particular person's tomb (who would have served as witness if it hadn't happened that way). And forget about the annoying detail that Jesus' enemies were concerned that his disciples would steal the body, so they demanded that a Roman guard be set up to watch over it. If the body wasn't buried, why did they demand a guard at the tomb?

Which brings us to the question of whether his disciples stole the body. Shall we believe that the twelve men who fled in terror and denied their friend (lest they, too, would be tortured and crucified) now suddenly did an about-face? Now they summoned the courage to get together, plan a heist worthy of a *Mission Impossible* film, creep out at night, overpower the Roman guards at the tomb, and steal the body away? Why would they have done this in the first place? Because they wanted to fake a resurrection? They were as surprised by the resurrection as anyone else. Wouldn't you be?

Did they do this so they could go on and start a religion based on their faked resurrection? I doubt it. As Mark Shea has pointed out, the disciples

> don't act like any cult leaders we know. The records they leave behind do not show air-brushed photos of fearless, shiny, happy, faith-filled dynamos of apostolic courage, theological acumen, and intellectual agility . . . They show us a group

of men whose chagrined honesty compelled them to carefully incorporate into the public record the fact that they were snobbish, spiteful, cowardly, factional nitwits who were slow on the uptake, ambitious, blind, selfish and, when the supreme test came, quite willing to bolt and run in the hour of their Master's terrible trial. Compare this with the adoring exhalations of the North Korean press on the Manifold Virtues of The Fearless Leaders, or the flawless perfection of Stalin according to the Stalinist press of the 30s, or the Nazi hagiography of Hitler. The apostles make sure that their public preaching, and the public record, includes a faithful recitation of their many, many sins. Moreover, they continue to preach the Resurrection for decades, despite separation, persecution, poverty, threats, torture, and martyrdom (except for John, who had the pleasure of watching his brother James executed for his testimony.) In short, they speak and act like honest men, not like men out to make a buck or acquire power.[1]

What comes across with terrific force in the New Testament is that the testimony has been given by people who tell the truth, even about awkward facts not instantly advantageous to their claims. They come across as people who genuinely believe Christ was risen, not as people who lie about a body that they know perfectly well was stolen or eaten by dogs. For the rest of their lives (right through to their torture and execution), the apostles behaved like men utterly convinced that they had met the risen Christ. Indeed, so convinced are they that they include numerous details that, frankly, no liar would ever make up. For instance, no first-century Jewish liars would call as their first witness Mary Magdalene. For the Magdalene was incredible to a first-century Jewish audience on two counts: first, she was a woman; second, she was a woman out of whom seven demons were supposed to have been driven—a rather shady psychological profile.[2] The Gospels read like accounts by honest people who are stuck with the facts—including the fact that one of the first witnesses of the Resurrection was a woman of uncertain reputation.

There are a few other far-fetched theories that do not even rise to the sophistication or inventiveness of conspiracy theories. The first is that the disciples went to the wrong tomb, found it empty, and concluded that Jesus had risen from the dead. Would they do that? Probably not. They'd just say, "Whoops. Wrong tomb. Where did they bury him anyway?"

Even if the disciples had been so stupid, credulous, and imaginative, surely the rest of the cast members would have corrected them. Had Jesus been in another tomb, all his enemies would have produced the body and pointed out the disciples' foolish mistake.

Then we have the group hallucination theory. This one goes like this: "Jesus died and was buried, but his disciples all wanted him to still be alive so they all had a hallucination that they saw him." So five hundred people hallucinated the same hallucination over a forty-day period at different times and places, and all the hallucinations matched up? And we should believe in such a thing as mass hallucinations anyway? Is there any evidence that such things ever occur? Not that I know of. Not outside conspiracy theories.

Furthermore, these are very detailed hallucinations. The hallucination talks to them, invites them to put their fingers in his wounds, eats and drinks, conducts a Bible study, and has extended conversations with them? I don't think so.

Then we have the modernist theologian's answer. For the modernists, as one Anglican bishop explained, the resurrection was "not just a conjuring trick with bones."[3] In other words, there was nothing crudely physical about it, but instead, in some sort of wonderful way, the teachings and example of Jesus continued to live in the hearts and minds of his followers and this, if you like, is what resurrection is really all about.

Is anyone deceived by this naked emperor? The whole meaning of the word *resurrection* is that a body that was dead came back to life again. There are spiritual meanings to be derived from this fact, to be sure, but if there were no physical fact, then the spiritual meanings would be meaningless. Saying that the resurrection was not physical but a spiritual reality is like a woman on her wedding night denying her husband the consummation of their marriage by saying, "We needn't be quite so crudely physical as to have sexual intercourse. Marriage is, after all, simply a beautiful spiritual idea!"

The modernist theologian's wishy-washy explanation doesn't account for the simple facts of the whole story. Shall we believe that the apostles went on to follow lives of hardship, suffering, and deprivation—finally being tortured and killed—for what was merely a "spiritual meaning" or a "beautiful theological idea"?

When faced with the slow torture of crucifixion or being flayed or boiled alive, don't you think they would have said, "Hold on! All that resurrection Son of God stuff? You misunderstood! It didn't really happen! It was only a spiritual meaning! It was a metaphor! It was a theological construct!"

Finally, we have the biblical scholars' theory that Saint Paul and the gospel writers (who supposedly weren't really Matthew, Mark, Luke, and John but were other people faking their names much later) made up all the resurrection stories to bolster their new religion. There are too many implausible details to go into here, but the main obstacle to this conspiracy theory is that Saint Paul died only thirty years after the death of Jesus himself, and he reported that the stories he had told about the resurrection were facts he himself had received from others. If Saint Paul or the gospel writers had made it all up, there were plenty of eyewitnesses alive who would have corrected them—not least, the murderous enemies of the new religion.

When you stop to examine the different theories about the resurrection of Jesus Christ, you have to admit that they're inventive and interesting—like all conspiracy theories. In fact, if you're really interested, why not examine all the alternative theories and see if you can come up with one that fits the facts as we know them and explains things satisfactorily? If you can, write a book called something like *Unlocking the Jesus Code* or *The Easter Mystery Solved!* You will probably make a ton of money and be offered a professorship of New Testament exegesis at an Ivy League school.

If you take the time to think it through even a little bit, you have to realize that all the different conspiracy theories and imaginative stories are harder to believe than the simple explanation: Jesus of Nazareth rose physically from the dead and didn't die again. It was a one-of-a-kind supernatural event.

Now all we have to do is ask what we are going to do about it.

18

My Red Plume

The Eternal Flame

In the final scene of *Cyrano de Bergerac*, Cyrano—the romantic hero, the poet with the proboscis, the knight with the noble nose—comes to see Roxanne, the only love of his life. A log has been dropped on his head by a cowardly enemy, and he is dying. He finally admits his love for Roxanne and realizes her halting love for him. His words become slurred, and as he stumbles and falls to the ground on one knee, he sweeps his broad-brimmed hat from his head and he says, "Yet there's something still that will always be mine, and when today I go to God's presence, there I'll doff it and sweep the heavenly pavement with a gesture—something I'll take unstained out of this world . . . My panache."[1] And with that, he gasps his last.

His "panache" is the white plume on his hat. It symbolizes Cyrano's indomitable spirit, his flamboyant courage, his intelligent foolishness, his romantic bravery, and his noble love. If Cyrano had his white plume, I claim the red plume, for it is not the plume of my own spirit but the bloodred plume of the chevalier of heaven—Christ the Knight—the brave Son of God, who played the hero in this world, died a victim martyr for the truth, and rose triumphant over death. So Christ is pictured by Piero della Francesca rising naked from the tomb, bearing a red-and-white flag of victory as he tramples over the sleeping soldiers. When I see that flag, I see my red plume.

The plume is the Christian red badge of courage. It is the sign and symbol of supernatural power through which the Christian conquers. What I am talking about is the gift that the triumphant Christ left to this world: the supernatural gift we call the Holy Spirit.

This is triumphant and flamboyant language indeed—language worthy of the noble Cyrano de Bergerac. What is this red plume? It is an unusual energy source within a human being. It is not fire in the belly but fire in the heart. It is the eternal flame. It is the same creative power that called the cosmos into being. It is the power through which the Lord was made incarnate of the Virgin Mary. It is the power that brought Jesus Christ to rise from the dead, and it is given to his followers as a generous Lord distributes boons to his minions.

What is this red plume? It is an unusual energy source within a human being. It is not fire in the belly but fire in the heart.

In the New Testament this gift was pictured as tongues of flame coming down to light upon the heads of the first Christians. The fire touched their lives. It possessed them. It took them over and filled them with an indescribable but undeniable power. It was a power that transformed them from frightened fishermen to monumental masters who changed the world. This fire, this energy, this dynamic new force within might be described as Christ-life, and followers of Christ believe that they are given this supernatural element in their lives through the existential transaction called *faith*.

Faith for the Faithless

Mention faith to the dull unbelievers and it is not a red plume but a red flag. The alarm bells go off and they scoff, for there are few religious concepts more derided by the faithless than faith. "Faith," says the scientifically minded atheist, "is believing something for which there is no evidence. Such a concept," he concludes, "is impossible for people who use their brains." Or the cynical philosopher says, "Faith is believing in the 'God of the gaps'—when the believer has no reasonable answer to a difficult question, he uses a deus ex machina solution. He plays the 'faith' card and calls for divine assistance. This, too," the philosopher opines, "is unworthy, unintelligent, and unfair."

Then there are the misunderstandings of faith held not by the faithless but the faithful. That is to say, too many people of religion also do not understand faith. Some who maintain their religious duties also maintain their ignorance about the faith; they think faith is believing something that everybody really knows is a load of codswallop. So they trot along to church on Easter morning and pretend to believe the whole story, but they know deep down it is all a big fairy tale. However, by keeping up the facade, they think they are keeping the faith. We do not call this *faith*; we call it *hypocrisy*, *stupidity*, or *cowardice*.

Then there are those who believe faith consists of having a particular sort of religious experience—usually of the emotional kind. Perhaps they have seen a coincidental "answer to prayer" and this has sparked their "faith," or maybe they have felt sad at a sentimental song, then felt happy when they stopped crying, and felt happier because they knew that Jesus loved them. We do not call this *faith*; we call it *marshmallows* or *cotton candy*.

Finally, there are those religious people who think faith is ascribing to a particular set of doctrinal propositions and moral regulations. They have given intellectual assent the way they might click the box agreeing to terms of use for a website. We do not call this *faith*; we call it *dead, boring, yawn-inducing legalism*.

Faith is something different. It is a process that resembles the procedure used by any scientist or researcher. The first step is observation and inquiry. Individuals see the world around them and ask certain questions about it. They see the religious phenomenon. They consider with curiosity the question of the supernatural, or life after death, or the existence of God. They gather the evidence and begin to ask more questions. Then they propose a theory that answers the questions. They test the theory and gather more evidence. They listen to witnesses and study further. They go through this process with an open mind and a listening ear and a sensitive heart. They gather evidence and witnesses—not just from the intellectual aspect of life but also from the arts, from history, from ordinary people, from extraordinary people, from the workplace, the family, the community, and from as much of their whole world as possible. They listen further and refine their theory further. They take advice. They learn from the experience of those who have gone before.

> *Faith is something different. It is a process that resembles the procedure used by any scientist or researcher.*

Then they make a decision. They decide to commit to a belief and behavior system based not on insecure or sentimental or stupid or blind faith but on the evidence they have gathered. This intelligent and informed commitment we call *faith*. Furthermore, the commitment (as I have said) is not just an intellectual assent to a belief system or code of behavior. It is a commitment to a new way of life, a new way of seeing, a new way of being, a new way of believing. This commitment is sealed by the ritual of baptism, and through this ritual and this faith, people receive a new source of energy in their lives. They receive the eternal flame, the volcanic fire, the burning heart, the Christ life, the red plume.

Purifying Fire

This new life is like a furnace burning at the heart of the newly committed soul, and the image of fire is vibrant, for fire can be as violent as a volcano or as quietly intense as an ember. The fire within may burn bright and high at first, then die down to a white-hot burning coal. Whenever the fire burns in the soul, it does the work of fire: it provides heat, energy, and light. Heat to warm the soul. Energy to enliven the soul. And light to illuminate the soul.

However, be warned. Like fire, the Holy Spirit can only provide the light and heat and energy by consuming fuel. The fuel it consumes is everything that is fit for the flames within a human soul. Is there trash in your life? It will be burned up. Are there values of wood, beliefs of straw, ideas of paper? They will be consumed. Do you have trashy habits, rubbishy vices, garbage addictions? They will be burned up in the furnace, and the hotter the flames are, the better—for some trash requires high temperatures to be consumed. I should not need to add that this process will not be comfortable, but as the saying goes, "If you can't take the heat, get out of the gold foundry."

Be warned. Like fire, the Holy Spirit can only provide the light and heat and energy by consuming fuel. The fuel it consumes is everything that is fit for the flames within a human soul.

Once the waste is consumed, the soul is consumed by the fire in a different way. The life is consumed, but not the soul. The soul becomes the burning bush that Moses saw—aflame but not consumed. The soul becomes one with the consuming fire as a bar of iron becomes one with the fire. It is put into the fire, the heat enters the iron itself, the iron begins to glow red hot with the fire, and it becomes a living fire itself, the iron and the fire becoming one. So, eventually, is the soul infused with the divine fire.

That this is a possibility for human beings is confirmed by the lives of the remarkable people we call *saints*. The word means "holy ones," and *holy* means, among other things, "whole." These are individuals who are complete. They have become who they were created to be. This possibility becomes a destiny once the transaction of faith is completed and the Holy Spirit begins the fiery work of transformation.

Furthermore, this transaction of faith is an action for the whole of a lifetime, not merely one moment. It entails an adventure of conversion and transformation that costs "not less than everything." It requires a lifetime's commitment to the quest—the quest to find completion and the consummation of Love.

The Fire of Love

Now the romantic hero has gone farther than he thought he could go. He has penetrated the inner sanctum of the castle glorious. He has gone through the dark wood and down, down, down through the underworld and come through the other side to begin the ascent of the Mountain Purgatorio. He wanted to fall in love but he has fallen for Love. He went in search of his true love and found Truth and Love instead, and his heart burns with the unquenchable fire. He approaches the end of the quest, only to realize that it is the beginning of a new and deeper and more frightening adventure: the adventure of Love.

This is where the truly romantic quest leads—to love. And by *love* I do not mean erotic love. I do not mean sentimental love. I do not mean patriotic love. I do not mean the love of friendship or of family or even of oneself or one's faith. I mean a kind of love that both fulfills and consumes those other, lesser loves. I mean, not being in love, but Being in Love and Love in Being.

I am talking in riddles because now I am in a realm that is superlinguistic. It is above the normal modes of language, therefore the only language left is the language of love—the ridiculous riddle of poetry:

> The dove descending breaks the air
> With flame of incandescent terror . . .
> The only hope, or else despair
> Lies in the choice of pyre or pyre—
> To be redeemed from fire by fire.

Who then devised the torment?
Love. Love is the unfamiliar Name
Behind the hands that wove
The intolerable shirt of flame
Which human power cannot remove.
We only live, we only suspire
Consumed by either fire or fire.[2]

That red plume; that panache; that fiery Spirit; that fire of Love is both the motor and the destination of the religious romancer's quest. He set out alone from his comfortable, ordinary world to go into an extraordinary realm—the realm of adventure—and after finding the flame of the Christ life, he has one step more to make and one more realization: that he is not alone. Through his transformation he comes to realize that there are more—many more—like him, and they are waiting to welcome him home.

19

THE RULE OF RELIGION

The Secret Army

Any person who has viewed the idiocy, hypocrisy, cant, crime, and complacency of life must wish, at some point, to do a Don Quixote and set off on a mad but noble crusade against the wicked foolishness of the world. Do not even the meekest of souls long at times to be subversive—to set out on a quest of protest against the idiotic depravity and decadent pomposity of the world? Hasn't every simple, true, and honest soul longed to be an antiestablishment protester—to overturn all the smug, mad, and bad men who run the world? Haven't we all longed to be a revolutionary, a Luddite, a Franciscan, or an Amish farmer and live a life that is radical and countercultural? Alas, we too soon cave. We give in. We comply. We decide for drudgery, we sign on to be a drone or a dromedary. We opt for the salary, the insurance plan, and the job security . . . and we learn to keep our mouths shut.

The romantic hero, however, sets out on such a quest, happy to go it alone—realizing that his task is lonely and that he will be ridiculed, misunderstood, persecuted, imprisoned, and even slain for his efforts. However, the religious romancer, the serious subversive, the Christian Quixote, the saintly Cyrano soon discover that they are not, in fact, alone; they are accompanied by a whole ragtag band of freedom fighters who share the same subversive aims and wish to undermine the status quo in order to establish a state of grace. What I mean is that the Christian hero soon finds that there is an army of others who are on the same quest, and he is part of a secret force in this world that is billions strong.

The Christian hero soon finds that there is an army of others who are on the same quest, and he is part of a secret force in this world that is billions strong.

Those without faith often perceive the Christian church as a dull and respectable institution—like one of those clubs where socialites meet for lunch. They like to imagine that the pope lounges at the high table with the presidents and princes. They see the pastors mixing with all the respectable people—with homes in the suburbs, a pension plan, and pleasant, well-scrubbed children like everyone else.

The irony is that the very same worldlings who look down on the Christian church for being a respectable bastion of the established order also sneer at those church members who are clearly *not* part of the established order. Take them to a Holy Roller church full of illegal immigrants, and they will turn up their noses. Take them to the Bronx and show them a gang of young Franciscan friars in burlap robes, sandals, and long beards and they will howl in horror. Let them peek into a cement block church in the Appalachians full of hootin' and hollerin' snake handlers, and they will be revolted. Take them to a Catholic Mass where poor Africans are singing and beating drums and dancing and they will tremble with distaste and dismay.

What they cannot see is the reality of the Christian church. Beneath the outward appearances, all true followers of Christ the Carpenter are, in fact, members of an underground army. Its members may appear to be respectable, but it is a ruse. It is a disguise. That plump pastor with the smile, the suit, and the big Bible? He's not there to support the expectations of the respectable world. He's there to subvert them. He's a spiritual guerrilla. That demure Sunday school teacher with the sweet smile and the sensible shoes? She's a freedom fighter ready to lay down her life for the cause. That mild-mannered minister with the soft hands and softer voice? He's a rebel and a rabble-rouser. Even the scarlet-soutaned cardinals, the berobed bishops, and Catholic prelates in lace are part of the underground army, and the worldlings should be even more cautious about those who do not seem to be subversive, for they may be the most subversive of all.

When I say that these people are a ragtag group of freedom fighters, I mean their basic viewpoint is that the established systems of this world are rotten and won't last. The members of this secret army march to a different drum. They follow a different leader. They are citizens of another country. They are not materialists. They don't buy in to the philosophy that what you see is what you get. In fact, they believe that what you *don't* see is what you get, and so they sit lightly to the things of this world, and by virtue of their underlying beliefs, they undermine the establishment. Because they live for another world they don't really care too much for this world; and because they are dismissive of this world, they are a danger to the leaders of this world.

> *The members of this secret army march to a different drum. They follow a different leader. They are citizens of another country.*

All those who truly follow Christ on the quest are members of this secret army. Yes, that means old Mrs. Tomkins with her Episcopal prayer book, her poodle, and her blue rinse. Yes, that means gawky Henry Mattison, the sixteen-year-old Boy Scout with pimples, who is an altar server and knows how to pray. It means burly Mikael the truck driver, who laughs like a hyena and has learned how to smile through suffering. It means Janet, the sweet and ordinary housewife, who bears in her heart the courage of a lion and the perseverance of steel.

It includes all who bear the mark of Christ the King—the old and the lame and the young and the hopeful. It means the wise and the foolish, the rich and the poor. It means believers from every race and language and nation on earth. It means all of them. Every single member of the church—in every denomination, from the little hokey one-roomed hut to the grandest Catholic cathedral. Each one who has faith and is baptized belongs to this great invisible army.

If the powers of the world could just once get a glimpse of the numbers and the power of this hidden force, they would tremble, and if they could ever get a glimpse of the invisible cohorts—the radiant and victorious souls who have died and gone before—they would not sleep at night for the terrors of their vision.

This is what is meant by the term "the church militant," for it is an army made up of countless individuals all empowered by the eternal flame, all bearing the red plume, all "charged with the grandeur of God."[1] This army fights the powers of the world with the invincible weapons of obedience, humility, wisdom, love, prayer, and faith. Those who really believe do not fear those who can destroy the body. They fear only those who can destroy the soul. Their commitment and their souls' lives are a greater loyalty than any general or president or prime minister can command. If you think I am exaggerating or that I am bluffing, simply read again the world history of the last fifty years and see how often tyrants have toppled, corrupt regimes have crumbled, and powerful rulers have fallen in the face of the people of faith. The greatest revolutions in the last twenty years have been peaceful revolutions inspired by faith and guided by love.

This church militant has marched down the centuries, bearing the banner of Christ victorious, but there is a tendency today to downgrade this great army and even dismiss the necessity of membership.

The Rule of Religion

In our flabby age, the most common comment about religion is that it is not required. "I am spiritual, but not religious!" cries the sophomore; or one hears the comment, "Religions are human institutions. God is much bigger than all those rules and regulations!" The critics of religion have understood one thing well: that religion is about rules. The word *religion* springs from the word *religio*, which means "reverence for the sacred." But the word *religio* is derived from the Latin word *ligare*, which means "to bind." Religion, therefore, is not simply about reverence for the sacred or "being spiritual"; it also includes the idea of being bound or obligated—and this is what the "spiritual but not religious" find objectionable.

I sympathize. The rules of religion can be tedious and tiresome. They take some learning, and like all rules, they can seem inconsistent, inflexible, and idiotic. Indeed, many of the rules also appear to be archaic, anachronistic, and absurd. Why should the Amish be allowed buttons on their clothes but not zippers? Do Jewish men really need to wear ringlets, black overcoats, and homburg hats? Why were Evangelicals allowed to play Rook but not pinochle or poker? Will Catholics really go straight to heaven if they wear a brown, postage stamp–size cloth around their necks? If the Bible is the rulebook, why do we eat lobster and pork chops and hesitate to stone to death adulterers and witches?

This problem is made worse by very strict religious people who have mistaken the rules for religion. In fact, they have made the rules their religion. They have forgotten that the rules are only a means to an end; they are not the end itself. The rules of religion are like the rules of a game, the recipe for a great dish, the music on the page to play the concerto, the ladder on which to climb, or the map for a great journey. Yes, we may not understand all the rules. They may be out-of-date, difficult, or debatable, but the existence of rules points us to a strange truth: that in submitting to the rules, we learn the most difficult lesson—the lesson of submission. As in anything worth mastering, we do not make the rules; the rules make us.

The rules make us aware of a ruler. They make us conscious of something greater and more expansive than ourselves. The rules lift us beyond ourselves and remind us that we are made for better things than simply obeying that most tyrannical of masters—our own whimsical desires and ephemeral ambitions.

> *The rules make us*
> *aware of a ruler.*

The spiritual quest is the greatest, the longest, the strangest, most complicated and difficult quest of all. Shall we attempt this great adventure without a guidebook? Shall we expect to make progress on this most mysterious, risky, and arduous quest without a map? Shall we scale spiritual mountains, skirt spiritual swamps, and avoid cliffs of temptation and chasms of sin by being "spiritual but not religious"?

Those who follow King Christ and join his invisible army are called to great and daring deeds—not simply a stroll on the beach at sunset or a walk through the garden alone while the dew is still on the roses. To go on this great adventure is the soul's goal and the heart's homing. Shall we set out on the quest with nothing but a mishmash of mawkish sentimentality and a hash of hopeful longing? Shall we reach for the stars and give all to become a saint with no one to guide us and no chart for the journey?

No, indeed. To be "spiritual without being religious" is like playing tennis without a net. The rules of religion provide the map for the journey. The map has been written by those who have gone before us and who show us the way.

Brothers in Arms

As one cannot go on the journey without a map, so also one cannot go on the journey alone. It is no mistake that from the very beginning God said, "It is not good for the man to be alone."[2] From man's side God created a woman to go with him. From the two of them he created a family of followers. Down through history his tribe was a pilgrim people. It was through them that God revealed himself, and it was through their life together that each one of them was able to make his or her own pilgrimage to the promised land.

In every great story the hero sets out on the quest alone,

but he soon finds friends and allies. That is what the church is for: it is the fellowship of the ring, the band of brothers, the army of the united. Together in the church, we become not only the army of God but the family of God.

> *That is what the church is for: it is the fellowship of the ring, the band of brothers, the army of the united.*

But here we must stop, look, and listen. I am writing about a vast united army of the Lord, but we know there are many different armies. There are divisions in the church. Are they no more than different divisions in the same army? Are the different denominations no more than different battalions all fighting on the same side? Are they all the same and all equal? Does it matter which battalion you join and which division you fight with?

Common sense demands that it matters. If you are setting out on a great journey, do you not wish for the best and most detailed map? If you are signing up for war, do you not wish to be trained by the most seasoned warriors, the most skilled soldiers, and the troops with the most experience and expertise?

How shall one find this best, fullest, and most complete battle battalion? That is another quest in itself, for the best and fullest army may not look at first to be the most spick-and-span. This quest, like the great quest itself, is full of mystery and marvels. Things are not what they seem. The shiny, smiling, "successful" soldiers may turn out to be no more than spit and polish, while the ragtag band of rebels may turn out to be the toughest, shrewdest, and wiliest fighters of all. All that glitters is not gold, and all that is gold does not glitter. The ones who seemed saintly may turn out to be sinners, and the ones you condemned as sinners may, in the end, be the saints.

The quest is mysterious, and the farther you go on the quest, the more mysterious it becomes. The romance of religion takes you into foreign parts and strange places. The spiritual journey will lead you into realms you have never visited before, and therefore the farther you go, the more important it is to have sound rules to help you find the way and strong friends to help you on the journey. As you travel, you realize that the rules of the religion have not been wasted. They are the very structures and strictures that have sped you on the way. You learn that you cannot live without them any more than the musician could profess to play the concerto without first having learned to master the music on the page.

This is the endpoint of the romance of religion: the romance is the rule and the rule is the romance of religion. The end point of the rule of religion is not to restrain the soul but to set it free. It is to be like the music student who has practiced and so been made perfect. He has learned his lessons, struggled with the score, battled with teachers, hammered out the notes, and memorized the music. He has mastered the music by being mastered by the music. He has overcome all obstacles, and through the hard discipline and the rule of the music, he has blossomed into a maestro.

Then, one day, he steps out onto the stage and walks to the piano and plays the concerto with a freedom that could only be forged through discipline and a beauty that is born in battle.

20

Riding into the Sunset

The End of All Things

There is something poetic about westerns ending with the hero riding into the sunset. After all, the sun sets in the west, and the best westerns (and I don't mean hotels) are movies in which the hero is on a quest, so it's fitting that he rides farther into the west. As he rides into the west, we know that he is ending one adventure and beginning another. The west has always been the land of adventure, the land beyond the horizon, the last frontier, the land of promise, hopes, and dreams. Those who sailed into the west from Europe were never seen again. There the world ended. "There be dragons." There in the west were strange, unknown lands inhabited by savages and strange and beautiful beasts. There is where the wild things are. The lonesome cowboy riding into the sunset is only a different version, therefore, of sailing into the west.

At that point in the great romance, we realize that the hero must ride into the sunset because his own sun is setting. That is to say, his day is ending. By going on the adventure, by setting out on the quest, he has become someone else. The old man has died. Behold, all things have become new. The hero has learned his lessons. He has grown up into the person he was supposed to be. He has reached maturity. He's ready to go home. We see this transformation in movies all the time. The professionals call it a "character arc." The scriptwriter shadows the main plot with a subplot, which is all about the hero's inner growth. This inner plotline runs parallel to the main plotline, which is always about action and conflict in the visible world. However, despite the explosions and chase scenes, the pitfalls and pratfalls, the love affairs and gunfights and fistfights, the audience is really most interested in the inner journey of the hero. Yes, they want to see him defeat the bad guy, find the treasure, and get the girl, but they are more interested to see if, through the adventure, the hero grows up, overcomes his faults, understands his weaknesses, and triumphs over his inner demons. This is what makes a true hero in the movies, and only this sort of hero gets to ride into the sunset at the end.

This is also the end of the romance of religion, for as I have said from the beginning, the Christian faith is an adventure like none other, and unless you understand that, you have not begun to understand anything at all. The romance of religion is the romance of inner transformation. The plotline in the visible world—the choices we make, the beliefs we choose, the person we marry, the children we have, the job we do, the god we worship—all of these mundane and quotidian decisions are simply the means through which we grow as human beings. We set out on the great adventure to accomplish some great task, but the really great task is not to do heroic things but to become a hero.

> *The Christian faith is an adventure*
> *like none other, and unless you*
> *understand that, you have not begun*
> *to understand anything at all.*

Transformation Forever

The purpose of our romance is total transformation—not into something other than what we are but into something more than what we are. The goal is to be transformed not into somebody else but into who we were originally intended to be. The ancient theologian Irenaeus wrote, "The glory of God is the human person fully alive."[1] What he meant is that God radiates the abundance of his joy whenever any human being reaches the point of fulfillment. Whenever a human being reaches his full potential and becomes all that he was meant to be, God is not only happy but he radiates glory the way an artist radiates joy at the completion of his finest work or the way a mother radiates joy at the birth of a much-loved child.

This transformation of the human being is a process of refinement that includes the whole person. If we are created in God's image, then God, who is a holy trinity, should be reflected in who we are, and so it is that we are made up of body, mind, and spirit. All three aspects of our personality are intertwined in the unity that is our human person. We mistakenly think that we are bodies with souls inside—as if our bodies were vehicles for the eternal part of us we call *soul*. We are not bodies with souls or souls inside bodies. We are a trinity in inexplicable unity—a body-mind-spirit.

Can we separate the body from the mind? No. The mind is not only in the brain. It runs through the whole of the body. Can we separate the soul from the mind? No. The soul does not reside in any particular organ of the body. The body is infused with soul as water is infused with tea. Can we separate the body from the mind and the soul? No. The body has mind and soul running through it—enlivening every cell and coursing through every vessel. Instead we are a marvelous unity of body, mind, and spirit, and all three must be transformed if we are to ride off into the sunset.

The transformation of all three aspects of the human person takes place through the adventure of religion. That's the point of religion. We thought it was to learn Bible stories or the right doctrines or to do good deeds or even to worship God and give him glory, but if "the glory of God is a human being fully alive" then we best give God glory not just by worship or good works or learning things about him or prayer or being good boys and girls. We best give glory to God by becoming human beings that are fully alive, and the way we become fully alive is by oiling the armor, dusting off the broad-brimmed hat, sharpening the sword, saddling up the horse, and embarking on the great adventure. It's deciding to be a religious romantic and setting out on the quest—to dream the impossible dream, to choose all or nothing, to fight dragons, to tilt at windmills, to brandish the sword at invisible enemies, to stumble and fall and get up again, to woo and rescue fair maidens, to love life, to bear our wounds with dignity, know our faults, repent of our sins, endure insults in silence, beat the bad guys, win the treasure, and then, at last, to ride into the sunset.

Everyday Adventures

It is easy to think that we must, therefore, do some great heroic act, but the lives of the saints—and these are the human beings who are most fully alive—show us that the great adventure can be lived within the confines of ordinary life. We may be called to do great deeds, or we may be called to do small deeds with greatness.

I remember looking out the window one day when I lived in a town where there were many retirement homes. I was on the third floor of a tall house and I saw Hilda walking down the street. Hilda was a woman in her late sixties—a widow. She was crippled. Her left leg was bowed out like a semicircle. She wore special shoes, and crumpled cardigans and thick glasses too. I spotted Hilda marching down the street in her funny galumphing gait, and I saw she was carrying a bag in her hand. I knew that she was off on one of her outings to visit one of her "old ladies." Hilda—never waiting to be asked or thanked—made cupcakes every morning and spent the afternoon marching around town, visiting women who were older and sadder and lonelier than she was to drink tea and eat cakes.

Suddenly I had a vision of who Hilda really was. I have spoken about secret armies and ragtag troops of freedom fighters, and I saw that Hilda was one of the foot agents of the Lord. She was an ordinary hero. Old Hilda, marching along with her cupcakes, was a valiant warrior—a member of the infantry of the infant King. She showed me humanity reaching its full potential. She showed me a human being simple and free and fully herself. She was doing what she was meant to do with grit and good humor and hard work and faith. She showed me a human being fully alive, and therefore she revealed to me God's glory.

This is the goal of romantic religion—for ordinary people to become extraordinary by becoming who they were meant to be. Not each of us becoming Hildas, catering tea and cakes, but each of us becoming who we are meant to be. This task, then, is the task for everyone in every way through every day. It is to see each day as one page in the great adventure. It is to see the ordinary life as infused with extraordinary opportunities. It is to realize that running parallel to the plotline of our lives, there is an inner character arc being developed. Each day, with its decisions, is a step in the quest. Each relationship is the opportunity for growth. Each decision—no matter how small—has an impact on the great adventure.

We may be called to do great deeds, or we may be called to do small deeds with greatness.

Heavens Below

We think of "heaven above," but what if it were really "heaven below"? What I mean to say is that heaven is not some dreamy place beyond the clouds, where everything is impossibly white and gold and clean and beautiful. Is heaven some sort of spiritual state of being that we cannot imagine because it is so ethereal and abstract and cloudy? I doubt it. I suggest that heaven, instead, is the fulfillment or completion of what we have experienced here on earth. If this heroic transformation I am talking about is the fulfillment of everything I was created to be, then surely heaven is also the fulfillment of everything this earth was created to be.

If that is so, what will heaven be like? I think it will be like everything good on this earth, but without the imperfections. It will be a condition of complete simplicity. All things will be natural there—as natural and free as a day in May. All things will be in their proper order—each person, each creature, each thing down to the last detail in its right and harmonious place in relationship to one another and to the Creator.

There will be peace—the kind of peace that we experience in the natural world when all is in harmony and there is a constant energy and dynamism but there is no conflict. We will experience that peace by being ourselves in exactly the right place, by being all that we were created to be in relationship with everyone else and with the Creator.

Finally, there will be love. Again—not love in the erotic sense, but the Love that moves the sun and all the other stars. This Love is the motor and dynamism of that West beyond the sunset. Saint Thomas Aquinas says that this Love is the energy force that binds together the three persons of the Holy Trinity.[2] It is the Love by whom all things were created. To be in heaven will be to be immersed in that Love, to live in that Love as a fish lives in water or a bird in the air. To be in heaven will be to dwell in that Love as the air we breathe and the sun that warms us. The book of Revelation refers to this Love as Light and sees that we will dwell in this Love and this Light—not in some abstract way, not in a way that is less real than this world, but in a way that is more real.

This Love and this Light will make this world seem shallow, flat, tasteless, and bland. It will be to this world what a full Technicolor 3-D movie is to a black-and-white still photograph—and more. This Love and this Light will be utter, complete, and simple fulfillment of all things. It will be Reality at last. The adventure will be over. As we ride into the West—as we sail over the sea and into the sunset—we will know that sweet Reality which is the destination, the end, and the purpose of the Romance of Religion.

ACKNOWLEDGMENTS

The Romance of Religion has had a long gestation. I began writing it ten years ago as the second volume of a trilogy following *The Quest for the Creed*, which is an examination of the Apostle's Creed. The third book will be called *The Sacred Sacrifice* and will examine the problem of evil and its resolution.

The first chapter of this book was presented as a paper to the Annual Chesterton Conference in 2006. I am grateful to Dale Ahlquist, the president of the American Chesterton Society, for the invitation to do so and the encouragement to keep writing. My fellow Anglo-American Joseph Pearce also encouraged my Chestertonian inclinations despite the warning that the only thing worse than Chesterton was Chesterton imitators.

I must thank rambunctious blogger Mark Shea for lending me great ideas in his rollicking defense of the resurrection, from which I borrowed heavily for chapter 17.

Thanks also go to Lorraine Murray and Ruth Ballard for reading the first versions of the manuscript and offering wise and sharp comments. Thanks, too, go to my friend and colleague Richard Ballard for his indulgence and support while I pursue my call to scribble.

Matt Baugher was a surprise supporter, and I thank him for his enthusiasm, commitment, and advice. Meaghan Porter and her team provided fantastic and professional advice, enthusiasm, and attention to detail. Thanks!

I offer a solemn thanksgiving to my ancient and most venerable friend Benedict and my little sister Therese for their prayer support. I also wish to thank others from that cloud of witnesses: Gilbert, Jack, Bishop Francis, Father George, Father Gerard, and the Old Possum.

I thank my parents for a solid, Christian, Bible-based foundation for life. Finally, I wish to thank my children, Benedict, Madeleine, Theo, and Elias, for tolerating the extra hours I spend in my study—and last but not least, my wife, Alison, who has sat beside me for a roller-coaster ride of over twenty years that improves every day. This is for Alison . . . at last.

With thanks and blessings,
Dwight Longenecker
August 2013

NOTES

Introduction: Respectability and the House of Horrors
1. Henry W. Baker, "The King of Love My Shepherd Is," *Hymns Ancient and Modern* (London, 1868).
2. Matthew 23:33 NKJV; John 8:44; Mark 9:44 (also vv. 46, 48) KJV. The verse from Mark actually reads, "Where their worm dieth not, and the fire is not quenched."
3. 2 Corinthians 12:10, author's paraphrase; 1 Corinthians 1:25, author's paraphrase; 1 Corinthians 15:55 NLT.

Chapter Two: All er Nuthin'
1. Oscar Hammerstein II and Richard Rodgers, "All Er Nuthin'," *Oklahoma!*, 1943.
2. T. S. Eliot, "Little Gidding," *The Four Quartets* (New York: Harcourt, 1943), 138.
3. Eliot, "East Coker," *The Four Quartets*, 126.

Chapter Four: Of Whirlwinds, Words, and Other Worlds
1. Matthew 18:3, author's paraphrase.
2. See William Blake, "Auguries of Innocence," *The Poetical Works of William Blake*, ed. John Sampson (New York: Oxford UP, 1914), 171.
3. John 1:1 and Acts 17:28, author's paraphrase.

Chapter Five: Either the Ethereal or the Real
1. C. S. Lewis, *Out of the Silent Planet* (1938; repr., New York: Scribner, 2003).

2. David Bohm, *The Essential David Bohm*, ed. Lee Nichol (New York: Routledge, 2003), 152.

3. Matthew 10:34 RSV.

Chapter Seven: Ideals, Ideologies, and Idols

1. Sheldon Harnick and Jerry Bock, "To Life," *Fiddler on the Roof*, 1964.

2. See e. e. cummings, "i thank You God for this most amazing," *E. E. Cummings: Complete Poems 1904–1962*, ed. George J. Firmage, rev. ed. (New York: Liveright, 1994), 663.

Chapter Eight: Beatrice, Beasts, and Beauty

1. Arthur Schopenhauer, *The World as Will and Idea*, vol. 1, trans. R. B. Haldane and J. Kemp (London: Kegan Paul, Trench, Trübner & Co, 1909; repr. Project Gutenberg, 2011), ebook, 88, http://www.gutenberg.org/files/38427/38427 -pdf.pdf.

Chapter Nine: Hollywood Heroes and Harlequin Romance

1. John 15:13 RSV.

2. Dante, *The Divine Comedy*, "Paradiso," canto 33, line 145. The translation is from Dorothy Sayers and Barbara Reynolds, *The Comedy of Dante Alighieri: Paradise* (New York: Penguin, 1962).

Chapter Ten: Truth, Treasure, Maps, and Traps

1. John 18:38 NKJV.

2. John 14:6, author's paraphrase.

Chapter Eleven: Hobbit Holes and the Holy

1. J. R. R. Tolkien, *The Hobbit* (1937; repr. New York: Del Rey, 2012), 1.

2. Luke 5:4, author's paraphrase.

3. Eliot, "East Coker," *The Four Quartets*, 126.

Chapter Twelve: Paganism, Poetry, and Pointers

1. C. S. Lewis, *The Lion, the Witch and the Wardrobe* (1950; repr. New York: HarperCollins, 1998), 79.

Chapter Thirteen: Miracles and Magic in Dust and Dirt

1. William Norman Ewer, *Week-End Book*, eds. Vera Mendel and Francis Meynell (Edinburgh: Harrap, 1924), 117.
2. Deuteronomy 26:5 NIV.

Chapter Fourteen: Of Gods, Girls, and Glory

1. Washburn Hopkins, *Origin and Development of Religious Belief* (New Haven: Yale, 1923), 353.

Chapter Fifteen: Superman or Son of Man?

1. Colossians 1:15–17 NIV.
2. Galatians 4:4 ESV.
3. John 1:1, 3, 14 NIV.
4. John 10:11 NIV.
5. Ezekiel 34.
6. Job 9:8 NCV.
7. C. S. Lewis, *Mere Christianity* (New York: Harper Collins, 1952; repr. 2012), 52.

Chapter Sixteen: The Sacred Sacrifice

1. John 3:16.
2. The phrase "dart of longing love" is found in the anonymous work "The Cloud of Unknowing." *The Cloud of Unknowing and Other Works*, trans. A. C. Spearing (New York: Penguin, 2001), 35.

Chapter Seventeen: Conspiracy, Hearsay, and History

1. Mark Shea, "If Christ Has Not Been Raised . . ." Mark Shea. com, 2003, accessed May 15, 2013, http://www.mark-shea.com /resurrection.html.
2. Mark 16:9.
3. Associated Press, "Bishop Compares Resurrection to Conjuring Trick," *Toledo Blade*, October 28, 1984, A24.

Chapter Eighteen: My Red Plume

1. Edmond Rostand, *Cyrano de Bergerac*, trans. Carol Clark (New York: Penguin, 2006), act 5, scene 6, lines 309–14.
2. T. S. Eliot, *The Four Quartets* (New York: Harcourt, 1971), 143–44.

Chapter Nineteen: The Rule of Religion

1. Gerard Manley Hopkins, "God's Grandeur," *Poems* (London: Humphrey Milford, 1918; Bartleby.com, 1999), http://www.bartleby.com/122/7.html.
2. Genesis 2:18 NIV.

Chapter Twenty: Riding into the Sunset

1. Quoted in Allen Fitzgerald, ed., *Augustine Through the Ages* (Grand Rapids: Eerdmans, 1999), 456.
2. Thomas Aquinas, *Summa Theologica*, first part, question 20, article 1, http://www.newadvent.org/summa/1020.htm.

ABOUT THE AUTHOR

DWIGHT LONGENECKER has served as a parish priest; a chaplain at Kings College, Cambridge; and a country parson on the Isle of Wight. A speaker and broadcaster, he has written sixteen books and countless articles for websites, magazines, and papers in the United States and Great Britain. His blog, *Standing on My Head*, has been voted one of the top religious blogs in the country. He holds a degree in theology from Oxford University and currently serves a local parish in Greenville, South Carolina.